Pressure Group Politics

THE CASE OF THE
BRITISH MEDICAL ASSOCIATION

HARRY ECKSTEIN

Ruskin House

GEORGE ALLEN & UNWIN LTD
MUSEUM STREET LONDON

PRINTED IN GREAT BRITAIN
in 10 *on* 11-*pt. Plantin type*
BY C. TINLING AND CO. LTD
LIVERPOOL, LONDON AND PRESCOT

PRESSURE GROUP POLITICS

TO
S. H. BEER

PREFACE

I have envisaged this study as a gradual transition from the abstract to the concrete. Chapter I outlines a large number of hypotheses regarding the operation of pressure groups in any political system and isolates three crucial determinants of their activities, distilled from these hypotheses. Chapter II describes, still in rather broad terms, the situation of the British Medical Association as a pressure group in light of these three determinants. The next two chapters give a more detailed description and analysis of the character and effectiveness of the Association's political activities, and the two chapters after that present a detailed account of two actual negotiations, making the abstractions and generalizations of the preceding chapter as concrete as the sources permit. In the final chapter I return to certain broad theoretical problems to which the case-study is relevant but which it is not designed to illuminate directly.

It is hardly necessary to say that this plan of presentation has been adopted because I feel that the broad generalizations of Chapter I help one to find the more significant data of the Association's political life, while the details of the later chapters provide evidence of some sort for the generalizations. In the process of research the generalizations and details were not of course put together independently but worked out through constant cross-reference, the generalizations being made to reflect the details, the details arranged so as to illustrate the generalizations. I feel that this is no methodological hocus-pocus, but the right way to proceed in empirical analysis. The constant reconsideration of generalizations in terms of data and the selection of data in terms of generalizations is the heart and soul of systematic research, and both should be done quite consciously.

In compiling the hypotheses in Chapter I, however, I have drawn not only on my empirical knowledge of the BMA but also the theoretical works on pressure groups of other writers, chiefly David B. Truman and S. H. Beer. In any case, Chapter I may be read without reference to the case-study on which most of it is based, as an attempt to put together a 'theoretical framework' for the study of pressure group behaviour (but one which attempts, as much as is safe, not to retrace ground already made familiar by Truman). It applies to pressure groups in general, and therefore includes some generalizations not immediately pertinent to the BMA; it would be too much of a good thing if a single pressure group allowed us to say all there is to say in a general theory of pressure group behaviour. Hence also the data contained in the subsequent chapters are not intended as any sort of 'proof' of the generalizations, but only as illustrations. They constitute a case-study, and nothing more: evidence, not validation.

How does this study fit into other recent writings about pressure groups? Political scientists are aware that there has appeared in the last year or two a good deal of programmatic writing on ways to study pressure groups so as to make possible the wide comparative analysis of such groups. The most important and useful of these writings, it seems to me, is the report prepared by Gabriel A. Almond, of the Committee on Comparative Politics of the Social Science Research Council, entitled 'A Comparative Study of Interest Groups and the Political Process' (*American Political Science Review*, March 1958). My own study does not use Almond's report as a model, chiefly because I read it only after preparing the draft; in any case, I feel that the study is quite sufficiently relevant to Almond's concerns as it stands and that certain useful elements of it would be lost if it were recast entirely to fit the Almond mould, purely for the sake of more obvious 'cumulativeness' in pressure group studies.

The Almond report argues that the comparative study of interest groups is useful primarily because it links the elements of social structure and culture to political analysis. It suggests that the primary purpose of the study of interest groups should be to study the form of pressure group activity in various societies, how it is determined by elements of social structure, culture and political structure, and how such activity is translated into political choices. The present study does deal with the effects of certain elements of social structure, culture and political structure on the behaviour of pressure groups in general and the British Medical Association in particular, at any rate in so far as I have considered these factors relevant. It also deals with other variables which seem to me to be significant as determinants of pressure group activity, the most important of these other determinants being the pattern of policy in a society. About this Almond has nothing to say, and I suspect that his silence is due to one of the most ancient and most dubious postulates of pressure group theory: that policy is always the result of the interplay of group pressures rather than a determinant of the interplay itself. It can, of course, be both; 'feedback' in social behaviour has become a familiar phenomenon, and one can clearly see it at work in pressure group activities. And just as the present study takes into account variables not discussed in the Almond report, so it is concerned not only with the form of pressure group activity but also with its scope, intensity, and effectiveness; the last, of course, might be part of what Almond means when he talks about the translation of pressure group activity into political choices.

Those concerned with the cumulativeness of findings in political science will certainly not find this study far off the path of analysis recommended for our guidance and for the sake of the systematic accumulation of material by the Social Science Research Council Committee on Comparative Politics and by the *ad hoc* group on the subject collected in 1957 at the Center for Advanced Study in the Behavioral Sciences. In so far as it departs from their recommendations, it does so mainly by way of adding analytical dimensions; and that, I presume, is all to the good.

In one sense, however, the study departs from, rather than adds to, the Almond model: in its basic terminology. The deviation is perhaps slight, but since it involves the most basic terms we use in pressure group studies, i.e. the terms interest group and pressure group themselves, it should be explained.

I do not wish here to enter into the old definitional controversy over what constitutes an 'interest group', potential or actual: whether such groups are constituted by attitudes, by objective characteristics (such as income or occupation), or by common aims regardless of basic attitudes or characteristics. I do make a distinction in my own vocabulary between interest groups and pressure groups. *Pressure groups*, needless to say, pursue collectively common political aims (by means other than attempting themselves to govern). They may do so simply because of subjective agreements (shared attitudes), as do most 'other-oriented' (unselfish) pressure groups, like the British Town and Country Planning Association or the American Anti-Saloon League. Or they may do so because of attitudes—generally, though certainly not necessarily, selfish—which are rooted in common objective characteristics, as in the case of the British Medical Association or the National Association for the Advancement of Coloured People. *Interest groups*, on the other hand, I define chiefly by objective characteristics. In interest groups there exists a high probability that political purposes will be pursued collectively, and normally this is the case in groups sharing objective characteristics. A slightly different way to put this is to say that interest groups are 'categoric' groups (Easton calls them 'groupings')[1] which are likely collectively to pursue political aims just because they have objective characteristics in common. Such groups *need* not always be involved in politics; but when they become engaged in politics they are a species of the broader genus 'pressure groups'. 'Interests' always grow out of objective characteristics, while political 'goals' may grow out of interests, but also out of values which are not reflections of objective characteristics. If groups having no 'interest' in common engage in politics, I call them (following Allen Potter) *attitude groups*.

These definitions, like all definitions, are arbitrary, but they seem to

[1] David Easton, *The Political System*, New York 1953, p. 185 ff.

me to have two virtues. They distinguish between things that ought to be distinguished (goals reflecting objective characteristics and goals reflecting purely subjective values) and correspond to the sense in which the term political 'interest' is generally used in ordinary speech. I can see no reason why we should call all political goals 'interests' (as does Beer)[1] or why we should speak of interests only when shared attitudes actually exist (as recommended by Truman),[2] without distinguishing the nature and origins of the attitudes. These recommended usages seem to me to stack the cards against a theory I consider false—that political goals are solely the result of objective social characteristics—but which I am not willing to read out of court by a definition.

Truman seems to think that we ought not to use the term pressure group 'scientifically' because it implies shady dealing and corruption. He suggests 'political interest group' instead. The point is hardly very important, but I demur; partly, because that term would make it difficult to keep apart subjective political goals and objective political interests; partly, because I feel, with V. O. Key, that 'the objectives of a pressure group may be good or bad'; and partly, because I do not think of 'pressure' as equivalent to blackmail. For reasonable men, the presentation of a reasonable case is a form of 'pressure' too.

S. E. Finer, in Anonymous Empire,[3] also makes a case against the concept 'pressure group'—and goes Truman one better by dismissing equally peremptorily the concept 'interest group'. Finer dislikes the term 'pressure group' for two reasons. The first repeats Truman's objection: to apply pressure seems to him tantamount to threatening sanctions of some sort, while many political groups merely argue cases or make requests. The second reason is that the term pressure group is too inclusive and one-sided: groups which seek to influence politics do many other things, so that the term 'pressure group' gets merely at one facet of their activities. The term 'interest groups' Finer dislikes because it is too exclusive a concept. Not all politically active groups try to satisfy their 'interests'; there are 'promotional groups' (attitude groups) as well: groups that espouse causes rather than press vested interests. What then are we to call such groups ? Finer suggests that we refer to them collectively as the Lobby.

I think that Finer's exceptions to the old vocabulary are well taken, but I do not think that we ought to agree to his recommendation. If 'pressure group' is to be read out of the dictionary because it carries (whether it should or not) the connotation of sanctions, surely we ought to read out terms like Lobby and Lobbyist too, because they carry, to my

---

[1] Beer and Ulam, *Patterns of Government,* Ch. 5.
[2] Truman, *The Governmental Process,* p. 33 ff.
[3] Pall Mall Press, 1958.

sensibilities at any rate (and I venture to say to those of most Americans), even more pungent implications. Lobbyists are people who try to get things unfairly, who intrigue and bribe and attack us subliminally; in America we make them register like paroled convicts or foreign agents. And even if we opt for the term Lobby as a collective category, how are we to label individual groups engaging in the Lobby when we are concerned with the part and not the whole (as I am in most of this study)?

It seems to me that we simply cannot solve the two problems which plague Professor Finer—how to rid ourselves of emotional responses to terms like pressure group (or Lobby) and how to label groups which carry on a wide variety of activities with a wide variety of motivations—by using a single word or two, invented or conventional. Surely it is no more misleading than anything else to use the conventional label, pressure groups, and to point out that we include under this label all groups which collectively pursue common political goals (excluding, as does Professor Finer, parties, i.e. groups that seek directly to govern); that these groups may be, and almost always are, engaged in activities other than political activities; that the goals they pursue may be interests or 'causes', and the means they use sanctions, arguments or petitions. Anyhow, that is how I mean the term.

A word about the footnotes, which are embarrassingly voluminous. Broad generalizations like those contained in Chapter I cry for examples and qualifications, some of which I considered important enough to incorporate into the text. In most cases, however, it seemed to me better to avoid tangents and complications by relegating them to the notes; however, most of the examples and qualifications contained in the footnotes are important and should be read if the argument is to be grasped in more than outline. In the other chapters I have used the footnotes, apart from the usual purposes of documentation, chiefly to explain terms not likely to be familiar to every reader and to present details which are worth knowing but which would have distorted and distended the narrative. This applies particularly to various aspects of the National Health Service, the most important area of the BMA's political activities, and to the composition of BMA bodies and bodies with which the BMA deals. Those who already know the structure of the Health Service and of the BMA can skip these notes; those who do not will probably get lost unless they consult them.

I am indebted to the Social Science Research Council for paying my way to England and enabling me to do research for this study; to S. H. Beer, who first made me realize that English pressure groups do indeed matter and helped me to formulate most of my ideas about them; to my wife, Joan Eckstein, who helped with some of the research and provided a discriminating sounding-board for my arguments; and to Professor S. E. Finer, Professor V. O. Key, and Mr Peter Self, who made useful comments. The responsibility for the actual contents of the study is mine, of course.

HARRY ECKSTEIN

Center for Advanced Study in the Behavioral Sciences
Stanford, California
December, 1958

CONTENTS

CONTENTS

I

Theoretical Framework

Problems

Case studies never 'prove' anything; their purpose is to illustrate generalizations which are established otherwise, or to direct attention towards such generalizations. Since this is a case study of the political activities of the British Medical Association it may be well to state at the outset the broad principles it illustrates. These principles are formulated in answer to three questions:

a. What are the determinants of the *form* of pressure group politics in various political systems ? What factors determine the principal channels and means through which pressure groups act on government and the character of the relations between the groups and organs of government ?

b. What are the determinants of the *intensity* and *scope* of pressure group politics ? 'Intensity' here refers to the fervour and persistence with which groups pursue their political objectives as well as to the relative importance of political activities in their affairs; scope, to the number and variety of groups engaged in politics.

c. What determines the *effectiveness* of pressure groups ? From what principal sources do they derive their power *vis-à-vis* other pressure groups and the more formal elements of the decision-making structure, such as parties, legislature and bureaucracy ?

At the end of the study certain other theoretical questions generally raised in pressure group studies are discussed, but the questions listed above are the main problems of the study.

Determinants of the Form of Pressure Group Politics
Channels. By the 'form' of pressure group activities I mean, first, the

channels of action on which such groups concentrate. The most important, and the most obvious, determinant of the selection of channels for pressure group activity, in any political system, is the *structure* of the decision-making processes which pressure groups seek to influence. Interest groups (or any other groups) become pressure groups because they want to obtain favourable policy decisions or administrative dispositions; hence, obviously, they must adjust their activities to the processes by which decisions and dispositions are made. To cite a very simple example: in Great Britain the National Union of Teachers is one of the larger and more active pressure groups on the national level, while in the United States teachers' groups play only a very minor role, if any, in national politics;[1] the reason is simply that British educational policies are made and administered by the national government, while in the American federal system this is not the case, except only in the most indirect sense. But this is perhaps too simple an example. Pressure groups tend to adjust the form of their activities not so much to the formal (constitutional) structure of governments as to the distribution of effective power within a governmental apparatus, and this is often something very different from formal structure; in the competition for influence they cannot afford to be deceived by political myths. Hence their activities are themselves one of the more reliable guides to the loci of effective power in any political system, whenever the 'political formula' of the system—as Lasswell and Kaplan call it[2]—does not indicate these loci correctly.

Not only the structure of the decision-making process but also the decisions which emerge from it—the *activities* of government—influence the predominant channels of pressure group politics, and this just because decisions have a reciprocal effect on the structures that make them. The most obvious example is the devolution of decision-making powers from legislatures to bureaucracies in this age of the social service state, both through the direct delegation of legislative powers and the indirect influence which bureaucrats enjoy over decisions still formally taken by legislatures.

Finally, the dominant channels of pressure group politics may be determined by certain *attitudes*, the most obviously important being attitudes toward pressure groups themselves. Where, for example, the pursuit of corporate interests by political means is normatively reproved

---

[1] V. O. Key, Jr., *Politics, Parties and Pressure Groups* (Thomas Y. Crowell Co., N.Y., sec. ed. 1947) does not even mention them. David B. Truman's encyclopaedic *The Governmental Process* (Knopf, N.Y., 1951) mentions the National Education Association (p. 452), but does not bother to describe its activities.

[2] Harold D. Lasswell and Abraham Kaplan, *Power and Society*, Routledge, 1950, p. 126 ff.

—where 'liberal' individualist assumptions[1] are deeply ingrained—pressure groups are likely to work through more inconspicuous channels and with more unobtrusive means than where corporate politics are normatively tolerated. But even attitudes not directly concerned with pressure groups may, indirectly, affect the form of their activities, at any rate if the attitudes have a bearing on the distribution of effective decision-making power. For example, a broad consensus on major policies—the sort of policies usually made by cabinets and legislatures—will tend to shift the major arena of political conflict, hence the major efforts of pressure groups, toward the administrative departments.

Basically, it is always the interplay of governmental structure, activities and attitudes which determines the form of pressure group politics (in the sense of channels of participation) in a given society. These factors may, of course, pull in different directions. Usually, however, they do not—chiefly (1) because the attitudes which bear directly upon a society's structure of decision-making (constitutional myths) and the attitudes which bear upon it indirectly (e.g. attitudes underlying governmental activities) tend to be integrated, and (2) because the activities of government and non-'constitutional' attitudes (such as attitudes on policy) generally have an important bearing on the decision-making structure itself. In Great Britain, at any rate, all three factors pull in a single direction: toward the concentration of pressure group activities on the administrative departments.

Pressure is concentrated upon the executive in Britain, first, because of the logic of cabinet government in a political system having two highly disciplined parties; such a system simply precludes any consistently successful exertion of influence through members of Parliament, or, less obviously perhaps, through the political parties.[2] Secondly, pressure is

---

[1] The term 'liberal' is used in accordance with S. H. Beer, 'The Representation of Interests in British Government,' *APSR*, Sept., 1957, pp. 628 ff.

[2] This is not to say that pressure on MPs is absolutely pointless. After all, they can ask parliamentary questions, press for adjournment debates, put down motions and amendments, make private representations to ministers and officials (i.e. use their prestige as MPs or their connections in the party), and exert influence within the party organizations. The very fact that pressure groups still find it profitable to 'retain' MPs indicates that Parliament is not yet entirely a dead letter in the structure of effective authority in Britain. (See, for example, S. H. Beer, 'Pressure Groups and Parties in Britain,' *APSR*, March 1956, pp. 5–6 and S. E. Finer, 'The Political Power of Private Capital,' Part II, *The Sociol. Review*, July 1956, p. 8. A comprehensive account of the parliamentary activities of British pressure groups may be found in the recently published work by J. D. Stewart, *British Pressure Groups*, Oxford Univ. Press, 1958.)

Pressure is also exerted to some extent through the political parties. Everyone knows that the Labour Party is in a sense an association of pressure groups: trade unions, co-operative societies and certain ideological societies. So is the Conservative Party; such business organizations as the Federation of British

focused on the executive because the broad scope and technical character of contemporary social and economic policies has led to a considerable shift of functions to the bureaucracy; not only that, but the decision-making powers usually exercised by administrative departments are, generally speaking, of much more immediate and greater interest to British interest groups than the kinds of decisions made in Cabinet and Parliament.[1] Attitudes, finally, lead in the same direction. There does not exist in Britain any profound prejudice against corporate politics, against the organization of opinion by 'interested' groups; this makes possible extraordinarily free, easy, open and intimate relations between public officials and lobbyists (using that term in a purely descriptive sense).[2] Attitudes in Britain also tend to shift pressure toward the executive in more direct and obvious ways: for example, because the lack of inhibitions upon delegating legislation gives to the administrative departments powers which legislatures more jealous of their functions

---

Industries, the National Union of Manufacturers and the Economic League may not be affiliated but are certainly aligned with the Tories, and there is considerable overlapping on the local level between committees of the Conservative and Unionist Associations and committees of trade associations. (S. E. Finer, *op. cit.*, pp. 6-12.) Nevertheless, parties also play a relatively minor role as channels of influence. They exist primarily to win elections: hence only groups having considerable wealth to contribute to party treasuries or a considerable member-ship strategically located in doubtful constituencies can hope to act successfully through them. At the same time, no party can really afford, for electoral reasons, to affiliate itself too openly and consistently with special interests; nor is it wise for any interest group to identify itself too closely with any party, since the party may only be in power occasionally—as the National Farmers Union, after a long alignment with the Conservatives, seems now to have learned. These considerations operate with special force in a real two-party system. In such a system the support of any special interest is likely to be of small importance to the parties, while, from the standpoint of interest groups, a given political party is more likely to be excluded from influence upon policy than in multi-party systems. The oscillation of power in two-party systems militates against any one-sided party alignments by pressure groups; hence the tendency of British pressure groups to assume a pose of political neutrality, even when they are clearly biased in favour of one party or the other.

Nevertheless, it is an index of the structure of effective power in Britain that pressure groups do concern themselves rather more with parties than the legislature. It is also an index of the structure of effective power within British parties that pressure groups concentrate their activities on the parliamentary parties and, to a smaller extent, the central offices (i.e. bureaucracies) of the parties, rather than on theoretically more powerful bodies in the party organiza-tion. (See H. Eckstein, 'The British Political System', in *Patterns of Government: The Major Political Systems of Europe*, eds. Beer and Ulam, New York, 1958, Ch. 12.)

[1] Farmers, for example, are likely to be rather more interested in the annual price reviews than in broad agricultural policies, doctors more interested in conditions of service under the Health Service than in general medical policy. That, at any rate, is what the behaviour of the National Farmers Union and British Medical Association suggests.

[2] See Beer, 'Pressure Groups', p. 6 ff.

than the British Parliament are likely to exercise themselves:[1] and because there has in fact existed in Britain a consensus on general policy,
shifting political conflict to matters of technique and detail, that is,
matters generally dealt with by administrative departments.[2]

[1] In Britain, after all, the process of delegating legislation hardly involves
delegation in any real sense, but rather a shift of responsibility from ministers
as leaders of Parliament to ministers as heads of administration. Hence the
staggering number of statutory instruments in this age of the social service state
and party government—from 174 general legislative 'rules' made by government
departments in 1900, to around 400 annually in the 1920's, to well over 1,000
since 1945, exceeding 1,500 in 1948. (See Sir Ivor Jennings, *Parliament*, 2nd
ed. CUP, 1957, pp. 498–99.) British Acts tend nowadays to be mere frameworks
for legislation. Of the 80 sections of the National Health Service Act, for example,
half require subordinate legislation, and these sections concern all the more
important aspects of the service, such as administrative organization and conditions of service; in the three years following passage of the act just under 150
statutory instruments were made under its provisions. (See *Butterworth's
Annotated Legislation Service*, 1950, code [26], issue no. 283.) In the USA such
blanket delegations of legislative responsibility are far less likely, if only because
a real shift of power from the legislature to the executive is involved.

[2] For a fuller discussion of this point, see Beer, 'Pressure Groups', Part III.
The arguments sketched above should not be interpreted to mean that British
pressure groups concentrate solely on the executive, nor that pressure groups in
other countries, e.g. the United States, do not also have close relations with the
executive. Truman's *The Governmental Process*, Ch. 14, presents a wide range of
data regarding the relations between pressure groups and the American executive, as do many other works, including Key, *Politics, Parties and Pressure Groups*,
Avery Leiserson, *Administrative Regulation: A Study in Representation of
Interests* (Chicago, 1942), E. P. Herring, *Public Administration and The Public
Interest* (London, McGraw Hill, 1936), C. H. Monsees, *Industry-Government
Cooperation* (Washington, 1944) and E. W. First, *Industry and Labor Advisory
Committees in the National Defense Advisory Commission and the Office of Pro-
duction Management* (Washington, 1946). The difference lies in the degree of
concentration, in the power wielded by pressure groups through their influence
at the administrative level, the intimacy of their relations with administrators,
and the extent to which they participate in decision-making or merely render
advice. The last of these points is discussed more fully below, pp. 22-25.
    It might be argued that this concentration of pressure group activity on the
executive is not really a reflection of the distribution of power among the formal
organs of government in Britain. Finer, for example, seems to take a slightly
different line (in *Anonymous Empire*, pp. 21–22). He feels that the preponderance
of contacts between pressure groups and departments is partly a matter of simple
good manners, partly due to the wisdom of finding out whether something wanted
is already authorized or not, and partly due to the desirability of keeping in the
good graces of persons with whom close contact is required in the implementation of policy and who may make things difficult on the legislative level, whether
they monopolize the legislative power or not. Of course, in all societies it is good
manners to consult parties interested in or involved in decisions; still, in Britain,
as we shall see below, it is a particularly flagrant breach of etiquette if policies are
made without close consultations between government and associations. As to
legal uncertainties, one might argue simply that they are so very great in Britain
because so much recent legislation has left details to be filled in by the departments, not because ministerial will as such is more important than parliamentary
will as such. Add the fact that the large range of consensus in Britain keeps most
political bickering within the range of administrative detail and prevents violent
—or 'important'—political controversies from arising, and one might draw the
following conclusion: the bulk of pressure group activity does take place at the

All this, of course, applies to pressure groups only in a general sense—to predominant and characteristic modes of pressure group activity rather than the activities of every particular pressure group. Whether any particular pressure group will concentrate on the executive or some other part of the governmental machinery and political apparatus of a society depends on certain factors additional to the broad variables I have sketched. For example, the power base of the group certainly plays a role in the matter. A group which commands a large number of votes will tend, other things being equal, to exert pressure on elected members of the decision-making structure; a wealthy group on party organizations; a group in command of specialized knowledge on the specialists in the governmental structure, chiefly the bureaucrats. But, to repeat, this is so *ceteris paribus*, not under all circumstances. It is very likely to be the case, for example, where there exists a relatively even distribution of power among representatives, party oligarchy and bureaucracy; or it may be the case where the group has only one power base which can be effectively brought to bear only in one direction. Both these cases, however, are unusual. In the ordinary instance, speaking metaphorically, the power base of the group will do little more than deflect the momentum of its pressure off the idealized path prescribed by governmental structure, activity and relevant attitudes. The ultimate aim of pressure groups is always to bring power to bear where it will produce intended consequences, and this makes the power structure of government a more decisive desideratum than the power base of the

departmental level; but it is not qualitatively important, however considerable in quantity; and it tells us nothing about the distribution of power between Parliament and Ministry for that should be measured only by taking account of really controversial questions of general policy.

This conclusion is not unreasonable; but I think that a slightly different view is more reasonable. Whether Parliament plays a very significant role in serious controversies or not (I think not), the fact remains that the bulk of the work of government is done on the executive level, precisely because of consensus, skeletal legislation and certain constitutional and normative attitudes. Serious controversies, at least compared with other countries, simply are few and far between, and that is one of the reasons for the predominance of the executive in Britain—although only one. The predominance of skeletal legislation is not due solely to circumstances (e.g. technical legislation) but also reflects the power of the executive, which likes to have a relatively free hand. And why should groups be so anxious not to get on the wrong side of the departments if the departments did not have crucial powers over affairs affecting the groups ? In other words, even if one cannot quite maintain that the executive dominates the legislature in each and every case, from the standpoint of pressure group politics the centre of power does lie with the departments, and clearly so. If there is an argument against the interpretation I suggest here it is, therefore, that it is over-generalized if applied indiscriminately to the whole of British politics, rather than the restricted area relevant to this study.

Other studies which bear out my point are Self and Storing, 'The Farmers and the State', *Political Quarterly*, vol. 29, no. 1, pp. 19–20 and PEP, *Industrial Trade Associations*, London, Allen & Unwin, 1951, p. 87.

group—granted that in unitary political systems like the British fewer alternatives for exerting effective pressure tend to present themselves than in polycentric systems like the American, and that in the latter, consequently, the power base of the group plays a more significant role in determining pressure group behaviour. Even in a system like the British, however, the direction of pressure may be seriously deflected, in special cases, from the executive departments. A group which simply does not have ready access to an executive department—which has no close clientele relationship with such a department—may be driven willy-nilly to seek its aims through other channels; so may a group which stands in a close relationship with a very weak department, when it wants a policy involving the interests of stronger departments; so also may a group pressing for a decision on some very controversial issue involving intense public opinion or high party politics, the sort of issues decided only at the very highest levels. These factors also work in the other direction. Where groups tend to press mainly on the legislature, the existence of close clientele relations with an executive department, or the fact that a group's business is not politically significant, may induce it to steer clear of parliamentary channels. But all these exceptions and modifications are just that, exceptions and modifications; they do not affect the general validity of the main point.

One should add that the factors which induce pressure groups to use certain channels of influence also have effects upon their internal organization and the means they use to exert political pressure. Pressure groups tend somehow to resemble the organizations they seek to influence. Take two examples, one American, the other British. Not only does the American federal system guide political pressure into certain channels, as in the case of teachers' organizations, but it impedes the formation of national associations as such. The American Bar Association, for instance, has a very small membership and was relatively late in getting under way compared to state and local legal associations. Why? Simply because training and admission to the profession—the two political concerns which most often lead to the formation and growth of professional associations—are controlled by state governments, not the federal government.[1] In broader terms, the formal dispersion of authority in government inhibits the concentration of membership in voluntary organizations, a fact with far-reaching consequences, because the 'density' of members affects many aspects of a pressure group's activities (such as its political effectiveness and the extent to which it can participate in genuine negotiations with public authorities).[2] In Britain we can see equally clearly the effect of informal

[1] Truman, *The Governmental Process*, p. 95.
[2] Elaborated below, pp. 34-5.

governmental power relations on the organization and tactics of pressure groups. As long as Parliament held the centre of the political stage—as long, that is to say, as political conflicts centred on parliamentary policies —interest groups tended not only to act chiefly through 'interested' MPs but to be ephemeral, one-purpose organizations, chiefly concerned with raising a large volume of public support for important legislative changes. Nowadays, however, they possess much greater continuity and engage in a much wider variety of political activities, for their interests are being constantly affected by governmental actions. The public campaign has been replaced largely by informal and unostentatious contacts between officials, and interest groups themselves have become increasingly bureaucratized (in short, more and more like the government departments with which they deal), for only bureaucratic structure is appropriate to the kinds of negotiations groups nowadays must carry on to realize their interests. The changing pattern of policy is not alone responsible for this. The shift of power from Parliament to the Cabinet and from the Cabinet to the administrative departments is equally important. These shifts have not been simple adjustments to new policies but are the results of many other factors, such as the professionalization of the civil service and the development of large, disciplined, national parties (paralleled by the development of large, national interest group organizations in place of the much greater decentralization of vested interest organizations in the nineteenth century). The striking correspondence of governmental organization and the internal organizations of pressure groups in most countries may of course be the result of a still more basic factor: deeply established 'constitutional' attitudes (an aspect of what Bentley called the 'habit background' of societies) which dictate forms of organization and power relations (structures of authority) not only in government but also in voluntary associations. For the present purpose, however, it is sufficient to point out the similarity and to suggest that it is a product both of social norms and calculations as to where and how group pressure can be exerted most effectively.

There is then a two-fold relation between the channels of pressure group activity on one hand and structure of government, pattern of policy and political attitudes on the other: structure, policy and attitudes decide the channels pressure groups will use predominantly to exert influence, and the nature of these channels in turn affects pressure group organization and tactics.

Consultations and Negotiations. By 'form' of pressure group politics, I do not mean channels of influence only but also the kinds of relations which predominate among groups and governmental bodies. Leaving aside the intimacy and easiness of these relations (which has already been touched upon), we may distinguish here between two polar extremes, consultations and negotiations, granting that most concrete relations involve both to some extent. Negotiations take place when a governmental body makes a decision hinge upon the actual approval of organizations interested in it, giving the organizations a veto over the decision; consultations occur when the views of the organizations are solicited and taken into account but not considered to be in any sense decisive. What decides whether one relationship or the other plays a significant role in government-group relations? The determining factors again are structure, policies and attitudes.

Structure is important because genuine negotiations can take place only if governmental decision-making processes and patterns of action within pressure groups are of a certain kind. Above all, those who speak for the public authority and those who speak for the interest group must be able to commit those whom they represent; otherwise their deliberations will have only a kind of consultative value, whatever their intentions. Negotiations, then, demand the concentration of authority on both sides, as well as the vesting of considerable discretionary authority in the negotiators. Indeed, the latter presupposes the former. Genuine negotiations between governmental bodies and pressure groups are not likely to take place when a decision must be obtained from a large number of bodies before it has force—as in the American separation-of-powers system—so that decisions are made in effect by negotiations among governmental bodies themselves; and how can there be any negotiations when the negotiators have no discretion, no room to manoeuvre, to make concessions, to meet unexpected gambits and pressures? From both standpoints, an effective cabinet system like the British clearly permits negotiations more easily than a balance-of-power system like the American. It is also necessary, of course, that there should be on the side of the group a formal organization that can speak for most of the members, rather than many competing organizations, or organizations unable to mobilize a sizeable majority of group members. This also is the case in Britain more often than in America.

Policies and attitudes in Britain reinforce the tendency of governmental and group structure to produce negotiations as the dominant form of pressure group politics. The policies of the social service state, for example, demand technical knowledge which, frequently, the members of some interest groups (doctors, for example) are best able to supply. In any case, they often require the positive co-operation of interest groups if they are to be effectively carried out; and what is more natural than to give the groups a direct voice of some sort both in the formulation and administration of policies which cannot be administered without their support?

Among attitudes making for negotiations between government and pressure groups in Britain three are of particular significance. One is the widespread belief (in this case both in Britain and America) that technical experts (practitioners) have some singular competence even in regard to the social policies and administrative forms that touch upon their fields of practice, competence which politicians and bureaucrats do not possess. The second (certainly without an American counterpart) is the persistent 'corporatism' in British social attitudes, the still lingering anti-individualist bias which Beer has labelled the 'Old Whig Theory of Representation';[1] by this is meant a conception of society as consisting primarily not of individuals but of sub-societies, groups having traditions, occupational and other characteristics in common. Where Lockean liberalism is the dominant political myth, decisions of government are supposed to be the result of conversations, as it were, between individuals (electorate) and sovereign (state); the intervention of groups is considered inherently pernicious or at best something merely to be tolerated.[2] Where corporatistic attitudes persist, on the other hand, functional representation—that is, the representation of corporations (in the sociological, not legal, sense of the term) rather than individuals —is not only tolerated but insisted upon; governments tend to be regarded not as sovereigns in the Austinian sense but, in the pluralistic sense, as corporations among many other kinds of corporations. Hence the frequent normative insistence on negotiations between government and 'voluntary' associations on matters of policy; in Britain, at any rate, a policy regulating, say, farmers, embarked upon without close conversations between government and farm organizations, would be considered to be only on the margins of legitimacy, whether highly technical in character or not. Indeed, close conversations are not enough. Note, for example, that in the debate on the second reading of the National Health Service Bill of 1946—the stage at which the most general policy considerations raised by a bill are discussed—the opposition hinged its case upon a motion alleging the failure of the Ministry of Health to *negotiate* the proposed Service with the medical profession; this despite the fact that plenty of talks (consultations) between the Ministry and the profession had taken place and that technical details were not at issue. And to the survival of the Old-Whig Theory of Representation we may add the concomitant survival of what might be called the Old Tory Theory of Authority: the tendency both in British government and British voluntary associations to delegate inordinately wide powers to leaders and spokesmen, to ratify decisions taken by

[1] Beer, 'Representation of Interests', p. 614 ff.
[2] For the best discussion of the origin and development of these attitudes, see Otto Gierke, *Natural Law and the Theory of Society*, Cambridge U. Press, 1934.

leaders almost as a matter of form, which affords such leaders a wide range of manoeuvre when they come face to face in negotiations.[1]

Consultations and negotiations are not, of course, the only 'practices' through which pressure groups act upon government. In fact, these two concepts may be useful for characterizing pressure group activities only in political systems which have two, not in the least universal, characteristics: a high degree of differentiation between pressure groups, parties and formal decision-making offices, and relatively great ease of access by pressure groups to the formal decision-making offices. Where these conditions do not exist, pressure group activity will inevitably assume other forms. In multi-party systems, where parties and pressure groups are not sharply differentiated (that is to say, where many parties are pressure groups that merely call themselves parties and sometimes behave like parties) decisions will often be made, not by negotiations between pressure groups and formal decision-making officers, but by negotiations among the pressure groups themselves. In such countries, the basic assertion on which contemporary 'group theorists' in political science have built their model—that politics is 'the allocation of social values through group conflict'—comes much closer to a full description of political decision-making than it does in countries where political parties perform their integrating function effectively and where the formal structure of decision-making represents something more than the myths of the dominant groups in institutionalized form. On the other extreme, where groups are effectively segregated out of the formal political process—prevented from having access to formal offices—the chief form of pressure group politics will be intrigue, or violence; perhaps, however, it would be better in this case to speak of the cessation of politics rather than of a particular form of it.

Determinants of Scope and Intensity

To discover the factors on which depends the scope and intensity of pressure-group activity, it is necessary to bear in mind just what sort of

---

[1] All this assumes that negotiations are in fact an important form of pressure group politics in Britain. But Stewart denies that the distinction between consultations and negotiations has much value in the case of British pressure groups. Why? Because, says Stewart, the decisions of a Minister are always subject to Parliament, preventing him from entering into binding agreements. (Stewart, *British Pressure Groups*, p. 22.) This, I suggest, is taking constitutional myths too seriously. Ministers undoubtedly find it convenient to leave themselves loopholes in negotiations with pressure groups by making agreements 'subject to the approval of Parliament'. But ordinarily, once a Minister had made a decision, it is, for all practical purposes, final. Parliament reviews few departmental decisions in the first place, and those it reviews it generally rubber-stamps. The Cabinet reviews few more departmental policies, unless important interdepartmental disputes are involved. The most effective limitations on the powers of Ministers arise out of such interdepartmental relations; generally, however, Ministers,

political activity pressure group politics is. As I define it[1] pressure group politics has certain peculiar characteristics which are very important. On one hand, it involves the *political* promotion of interests and values, that is, the attempt to realize aspirations through governmental decision-making; on the other, it involves something less than an attempt by the group to become itself the government, or even to seize for itself certain political offices which are vitally concerned with its goals. That, at any rate, is how we generally differentiate pressure groups from parties, or political movements, or purely political 'associations' (like the parliamentary associations which antedate the advent of mass parties in Great Britain). Moreover, pressure groups, normally, are not solely engaged in political activities; even in the case of 'promotional' groups (groups seeking to achieve not their own interests but what they conceive to be broader social values) political activities rarely exhaust the full range of activities of the group. Pressure group politics, then, represents something less than the full 'politicalization' of groups and something more than utter 'depoliticalization'; it constitutes an intermediate level of activity between the political and the apolitical. In accounting for the growth and development of pressure group activity, therefore, we must simultaneously account for two things which are, at first sight, nearly paradoxical: how groups come to seek the political promotion of certain of their goals, yet are kept from attempting to promote them by the capture of authoritative offices or from pursuing politically all their objectives. I shall concentrate on the first of these problems, the political mobilization of groups; the second is of less immediate concern to the present case-study, although I shall touch upon it at the end of the section.

The Political Mobilization of Groups: Policy. As governmental structure is the most obvious determinant of the form of pressure group activities, so the activities of governments are the most obvious determinants of their entrance into politics. British pressure groups have been so much discussed recently[2] for the simple reason that welfare state policies have, so to speak, generated such groups in large number (that is, transformed groups into 'pressure groups'), or, where they already existed, intensified the pressures they exert. This is clearly due to the fact that private associations now have much more to gain or lose from governmental decisions

---

when negotiating with pressure groups, will also be negotiating with other interested departments, so that agreements reached with the pressure group will be cleared in advance.

[1] See Preface pp. 9 ff.
[2] For a list of publications on the subject, see Finer, *Anonymous Empire*, p. 148. Add Jennings, *Parliament*, esp. Ch. II, sec. 4 and Ch. VII, sec. 1 and 2.

than in the past: farmers their incomes, doctors the conditions in which they practice, businessmen a host of matters, from capital issues to raw materials.[1] The state in Britain today disposes directly of 40 per cent of the national income; and that fact speaks for itself. We may regard political systems as amalgams of potential and actual pressure groups: groups which from a political standpoint are merely 'categoric' groups and groups which have actually been drawn into politics, chiefly through the impact of public policies, either policies actually adopted or policies which are 'threatened'. In short, we can usefully stand Bentley on his head to supplement Bentley right side up; if interaction among politically active groups produces policy, policy in turn creates politically active groups.[2]

There is also, however, a connection between the mobilization of pressure groups and governmental structure, and a further connection between the former and political attitudes, though neither may be quite so manifest as the influence of policy.

Attitudes. Attitudes influence the scope and intensity of pressure group politics not only because they determine policy but also because pressure groups generally require some sort of legitimation before they come into play in the political process. The obstacle to legitimacy may be internal or external, so to speak; it may arise either from the convictions of group members or that of non-members, particularly if the latter occupy positions of power, that the political promotion of the group's collective interests is somehow illegitimate. Trade unions, for example, play a more

---

[1] How much such groups stand to gain or lose emerges most strikingly in the pioneering *Report of the Committee on Intermediaries*, Cmd. 7094 of 1950. The Appendices, in which the relations between government departments and private individuals or associations are listed, are particularly revealing. Note especially the stupendous variety of activities for which permission and means (licenses, allocations, etc.) have had to be obtained from government departments. With the relaxation of controls since the immediate post-war period, departmental supervision over private activities has declined, but not much.

[2] V. O. Key cites a quaint example: in 1862 the United States Congress levied a tax of one dollar per barrel on beer; shortly afterwards the Brewers' Association was created to exercise, according to the preamble of its constitution, 'a proper influence in the legislative and public administration'. Many manufacturers' association were also organized in response to the first feeble attempts to regulate their activities. See Key, *Politics, Parties and Pressure Groups*, p. 177, and other works there cited. See also Truman, *The Governmental Process*, Ch. 4, *passim*.

The extension (or contemplated extension) of government policy is not, of course, the only factor which tends to draw groups into politics. Perhaps equally important is the desire to obtain legislation in order to impede rival groups or to regulate relations within the groups, e.g. the promotion by trade associations of retail price maintenance legislation or by professional associations of licensing regulations. Nor should one think of policies creating pressure groups in a sort of one-one relationship. Much depends on the objective characteristics and internal norms of the groups affected by the policies.

significant political role today than in the nineteenth century, both in
Britain and the United States, not only because they are larger and
better managed, but also because they are more widely accepted and
because they themselves are more reconciled to action within the
operative political system. To consult with trade union leaders is no
longer tantamount to conspiracy; nor do trade union leaders any longer
regard political participation in democratic government as a kind of class
treason, or as a trespass upon alien domain. Of course, the legitimacy of a
group is not absolutely decisive in determining whether it will play a
political role or not. Conspiracies do occur where negotiations are prohibited, but the difficulties in such cases are so great that 'illegitimate'
groups may find it desirable to leave politics alone, or impossible to
find channels through which to act. The attitudes which legitimate
pressure groups or deny them legitimacy usually constitute the fundamental political ethos of a society, such as the long prevalent liberal
belief that economic actors should act upon each other through the
spontaneously adjusting mechanics of the market rather than through
the political process.[1]

Legitimacy in this case need not mean legitimacy in regard to political
action only; a group may be prevented from taking an intense part in
politics by much more general attitudes: for example, a prejudice
against corporate organization as such. S. H. Beer has pointed out[2] that
the major occupational interests—business, labour, and agriculture—are
far more thoroughly and monolithically organized in Britain than in the
United States, and related this fact to the profound influence of liberal
'atomism' in America and the survival of the older corporatistic theory
of society in Britain. These differences in organization are marked by

---

[1] This point may be only of historical interest in Britain and the United States
today, since modern democratic attitudes legitimate almost all groups. (One can
think of exceptions—for example, groups supposed to be instruments of the
state, such as the military—although these usually have their private bureaucratic channels of influence, apart from influence by conspiracy.) But in the past
many groups—economic, religious, racial—have been more or less effectively
excluded from any political participation by virtue of dominant social norms.
Many also have had qualms about becoming tainted with politics: the British
Medical Association itself is a case in point. Throughout the nineteenth century
it tried, almost desperately, to remain purely a professional association, to the
point of provoking outright mutiny by politically-minded doctors. (See H.
Eckstein, 'The Politics of the British Medical Association', *Pol. Quarterly*,
vol. XXVI, no. 4, p. 345.) It is hardly necessary to mention revolutionary, e.g.
syndicalist, groups as a case in point from a totally different perspective.
Not only groups but also their interests require legitimation; indeed, *felt*
interests may be themselves functions of the value structure of a society. (See
John Plamenatz, 'Interests', *Political Studies*, February 1954.) Attitudes may
therefore restrict group politics either by ruling out all political activities by the
groups or by prohibiting activities of certain kinds or in pursuit of certain goals.

[2] In 'Group Representation in British and American Democracy', *The Annals*,
September 1958, *passim*.

differences in the groups' involvement in politics and administration. The sub-groups of larger societies may, however, have significantly different attitudes toward organization as well as political action itself. Thus, while it is true, broadly speaking, that British attitudes are more corporatistic than American attitudes—and that, as a result, British pressure groups 'even if compared with American examples . . . are numerous, massive, well-organized and highly effective'[1]—it is also true that British professional groups resist corporatization as much as, if not more than, their American counterparts. The British Medical Association, for example, has not until very recently (when special factors compelling corporatization have been at work) managed to outstrip the American Medical Association in proportion of doctors enrolled in it. This is just one facet of a much broader behaviour pattern; another facet of this pattern is the resistance of the British medical profession to all corporate forms of practice, in partnerships, group practices and especially health centres. Both reflect a profound bias against association which, in the American case, is much stronger in the realm of economic affairs, the area in which the liberal atomistic model of society was most rigidly applied in the United States. But such inhibitions against corporatization may be overcome. In medicine, for example, contemporary scientific development has made isolated practice almost obsolete, and this undoubtedly has had an effect on the willingness of British doctors to participate in corporate activities, both strictly professional and not strictly professional, however much some of the old biases may linger.

Attitudes may determine the intensity of group politics in still another way. Even when they permit intense political activity by a group, they may keep that activity from assuming certain forms, i.e. limit the group's range of political activities. Some groups which play a legitimate role in government may be prevented, by normative attitudes no less than considerations of expediency, from openly associating themselves with a political party or taking a part in electoral campaigns;[2] again, certain groups such as professional associations—may have deep inhibitions against anything that smacks of trade unionism (any sort of bargaining, for example); still others may be prevented by their internal ethics from using certain instruments of pressure, such as strikes and boycotts, or certain kinds of publicity—although changes in the situation of the group may also change such attitudes, as they may change attitudes toward corporatization and political action themselves.

---

[1] Beer, 'Pressure Groups and Parties in Britain,' p. 1.
[2] Note, for example, that the British Legion stopped its efforts to influence elections when threatened with the withdrawal of royal patronage because of its forays into party politics. See Graham Wootton, 'Ex-Servicemen in Politics', *Pol. Quarterly*, vol. 29, no. 1, pp. 34–5.

Structure. Of the three basic determinants of pressure group behaviour which I have stressed, perhaps the least manifest determinant of their political mobilization is governmental structure; nevertheless, it also plays a role. Key, for example, argues that a two-party system stimulates the formation of pressure groups because special interests cannot find consistent champions in any party which must continuously appeal to a great many interests.[1] That, however, strikes me as an over-simplification. The parties in a two-party system may themselves be composed of wings and sub-groups which consistently espouse certain interests, making them, as Key himself has pointed out, more like multi-party systems in fact than they seem in form.[2] This is certainly true of American parties. It may also apply to British parties, for both Labour and the Tories include certain enduring sub-groups which stand for special, chiefly economic interests. The point that should be made surely is that two-party systems do not encourage all interest groups to seek political channels outside of the parties but only groups having certain characteristics;[3] and rather than maintaining that multi-party systems discourage the formation of organized pressure groups because the parties themselves are freely available to special interests, one should argue that (just because of this) many 'parties' in such systems are themselves pressure groups in disguise, but pressure groups more fully politicalized than those we find in two-party systems.

Somewhat more persuasive is Truman's argument that certain groups are likely to pursue their goals through politics when the structure of government gives them important advantages over others and when they are in a relatively weak position on the 'market', that is, in spontaneous adjustment to other groups. His chief case in point is that of American farmers who have a relatively weak bargaining position on the market but are over-represented in both state and national legislatures.[4] Rural areas in many other countries tend to be over-represented too, which may help to explain the relatively great readiness of farm groups everywhere to seek out government interference in their market relations.

This argument may, however, be stated much more broadly: governmental structure affects the scope and intensity of pressure group activity chiefly because expectations of success govern the political mobilization of groups, and whether or not a group can be successfully influential is determined at least partly by the structure of the government on which it acts. Undoubtedly there are factors which enhance a group's chances of political success under any circumstances, but the

---

[1] Key, *Politics, Parties and Pressure Groups*, p. 177.
[2] Ibid., Ch. 10, *passim.*
[3] See note 2, p. 17, above.
[4] Truman, *The Governmental Process*, pp. 87 ff. and 107.

weight of these factors tends to vary according to the structure of decision-making in which they are brought to bear. This point will be discussed further below, in connection with a more general analysis of the conditions which determine the effectiveness of pressure groups. It ought to be noted here, however, that governmental structure may determine not only the influence of particular pressure groups (and therefore whether or not they will actually organize for politics) but also whether pressure groups in general can effectively translate their demands into policies (and therefore whether or not large numbers of them will be active, or whether political activity will play a large role in their affairs). I have in mind here the difference between systems like British cabinet government, which are highly effective in making decisions, and systems like the American or highly fragmented parliamentary systems, which seem more effective in frustrating them. The first kind of system is more likely to induce the political mobilization of groups than the second, if only because government offers them a reasonable chance of action—any sort of action; although, of course, everything depends in this case on whether groups actually want decisions to be made or to keep them from being taken. In the latter case, systems like the American clearly offer the greater chances, so that the distinction between active and inactive governments ought not perhaps to be made in terms of their effects on the political mobilization of groups as such, but in terms of the kinds of groups and aspirations they tend to involve in political affairs. In terms of sheer quantity of political activity one would certainly be hard put to find a significant difference between British and American pressure groups, but this does not preclude significant differences of other sorts.

Inhibitions on Political Mobilization. If certain attitudes, elements of governmental structure, and the impact of governmental policy, adopted and threatened, account for the political mobilization of groups, what inhibits them from mobilizing on a full scale once they decide to become politically involved? Clearly, the relevant factors are the ways in which groups define their goals and evaluate their chances in the political arena, and the extent to which an existing governmental apparatus appears capable of satisfying their demands without being changed or captured. Each of these considerations, however, requires some elaboration.

There are conditions when government itself, not the detailed products of government, is the primary concern of politics, most clearly of all when new states are in the building or old forms of government widely discredited. Such conditions are obviously inhospitable to pressure group politics, for they awaken much more profound political concerns.

Intensive pressure group politics then presupposes as its most fundamental condition a stable and widely accepted political apparatus—
political consensus. To 'press' upon a government is itself, in a way, a
form of commitment to it; profoundly disaffected groups will rarely stoop
to sully themselves by dealing with an abominated system. This
accounts for the curious impression one gets in societies widely committed to their governments both of intense politics and political apathy;
intense politics, because the society seems split into a myriad groupings,
loosely, if at all, associated, all busily seeking to exert influence, to
capture opinion, to enlist decision-makers; political apathy, because no
fundamental issues are ever raised and people seem remarkably uninterested in what looms, in other societies, as decisive political activity:
elections, for example The simple reason for this apparent paradox is,
of course, that political activities do not possess decisiveness intrinsically
but only in terms of what people want to be decided: if the chief political
question is one of the very location of formal power, then elections (or
violence) become decisive; if political questions involve less fundamental
issues—the detailed uses to which formal power is to be put—then
influence-wielding, i.e. pressure group politics, becomes decisive.
Consensus does not imply the cessation of politics, but it does imply a
shift of political concerns to issues best dealt with through the unobtrusive interplay of semi-politicalized groups; in 'consensual' systems,
therefore, fully politicalized groups will perform certain routine
functions but only rarely absorb primary allegiances. Lack of consensus
in a society will make almost every group join fully politicalized
organizations, or try to become themselves such organizations, or wash
their hands of politics altogether. Politics will become no concern of
theirs, or all of their concern. Whether it will be the first or the second
depends on contingent characteristics of the group and the situation
under which it has to operate: its size, the extent to which an existing
political state of affairs threatens it, the repressive power of existing
governments, and the extent to which its aims can be achieved outside of
politics.

Whether groups will define their goals as being fully political or, as do
pressure groups, only partially political may depend also on still more
fundamental characteristics of a society. A high degree of pressure
group activity presupposes logically a high degree of social differentiation. It is difficult to envisage intensive pressure group politics in
relatively primitive societies, not only because basic political questions
loom relatively large in them these days, but also because the vast
multiplicity of criss-crossing groups existing in more advanced societies
does not exist (at least to the same extent) in the less advanced. Group
politics in such societies tend therefore to define goals of very wide

concern, and associations tend to absorb wide segments of society; in such a situation group politics becomes almost by definition social politics.[1] The communications system of a society also plays a fundamental role, at any rate in deciding the very possibility of association as a preliminary to political mobilization. But apart from such absolutely fundamental and obvious (perhaps tautological) conditions, the extent of politicalization of groups is primarily a reflection of the degree of consensus among them. In that sense, the existence of a multiplicity of pressure groups is a sign of health in the political organism, not, as the muckrakers thought, a symptom of disease.

Within consensual systems, however, different groups have different propensities to act in politics, depending on contingencies like those operating in non-consensual systems. Very large groups and very wealthy groups may be encouraged to play a direct role in party-political conflict, as do British trade unions—although one gets the impression nowadays that their identification with Labour is a cultural lag from days of more profound political disagreements, and that they yearn (many at any rate) for looser forms of political engagement. Stable two-party systems also discourage full political involvement,[2] although such party systems may themselves be, at bottom, products of consensus. Finally, groups may become disenchanted in the process of pressure politics if the resolution of group conflicts is consistently against their interests—if, in the political market, their power to compete is small, due to their objective characteristics or the structure of government on which they act. In that case, however, they are more likely to become fully alienated from the political system rather than fully involved in it. In any case, the market of political competition tends to become so widely disjointed in highly consensual systems that almost any groups can get 'satisfactions' out of it; that is to say, groups which are relatively weak in absolute terms (in size, wealth, prestige, etc.) may, due to wide agreement, simply not have to confront significant opposition in their political affairs. Despite that, however, calculations of the chances of a group's effectiveness help to decide not only whether the group becomes politically active at all, but also the extent to which it carries its political activity. What then determines the effectiveness of pressure groups?

Determinants of Effectiveness
Factors determining the effectiveness of pressure groups may be

---

[1] 'Primitive' here is not meant as a synonym for non-western or industrially underdeveloped. It stands, in Dürkheim's sense, for a low level of social differentiation, and there are many ways in which societies may be differentiated. But the economic division of labour being one of them, economic underdevelopment is at least a loose and imperfect synonym for the term.

[2] See note 2, p, 17, above.

C

classified under three headings: (a) attributes of the pressure groups themselves; (b) attributes of the activities of government; (c) attributes of the governmental decision-making structure. Perhaps operative attitudes constitute a fourth category, since the ability of a group to mobilize opinion certainly enhances its chances of success in any political system in which opinion matters; but that is obvious and needs no elaboration.[1]

Group Characteristics. Certain characteristics of groups are likely to determine decisively their effectiveness under almost any pattern of policies or structure of government (popular government, of course): for example, physical resources, size, organizational cohesiveness, and political skills. Physical resources means wealth, first and foremost: wealth to contribute to party treasuries, wealth for 'buying' the goodwill of influential persons, wealth with which to advertise and circularize, and so forth. Other resources, of course, are useful too; for example, the possession by a group of a journal or newspaper, especially a popular newspaper, or (in a rather different sense of the term 'resource') the fact that it has members in influential positions. Among useful resources must be included also the prestige of the group: the capital of public support, so to speak, which it can command regardless of the substantive policies it espouses. Certain groups possess not merely legitimacy to participate in decision-making processes, but also a sort of special privilege to determine the outcome of these processes; this is true especially of groups possessing technical competence in fields where there is a wide gulf between the professional and the layman, although any high status and prestige can usually be converted into political profit, if only through the day-to-day influence of 'opinion leaders'.

The size of the group may itself be reckoned among its resources, although brute size is never likely to be of crucial account. Rather we should speak of the politically effective size of a group: its ability to make its quantitative weight felt. This is partly a matter of the other resources it commands—its wealth, prestige, whether it has easy access to public opinion and to influential persons—but still other considerations enter the equation as well. One of these is organizational cohesiveness, and this is a function of a great many variables. Does the group

[1] Truman identifies three factors which determine the extent to which a group achieves 'effective access' to the institutions of government: '(1) factors relating to a group's strategic position in society; (2) factors associated with the internal characteristics of groups; and (3) factors peculiar to the governmental institutions themselves.' (Truman, *Governmental Process*, p. 506.) (1) and (2) are grouped under (a) above; the determining role of public policy is not considered by Truman, at any rate not as explicitly as the other factors.

possess any formal organization at all? Is the membership split among a large number of such organizations or concentrated in an omnibus organization? Is membership perfunctory or the result of genuine commitment to the formal organization? Do members in fact participate in organizational affairs? Are their personal interactions frequent and persistent? Do they have important conflicting loyalties outside the group? Are their interests really compatible? Can the leaders mobilize disciplined and loyal legions in times of crisis? The answers to these questions will determine whether membership statistics can in fact be translated into influence.[1]

Among the skills which enable groups to achieve their political objectives we must therefore reckon the internal political and administrative skills of their leaders. Some groups, to be sure, are more cohesive than others in their very nature: if, for example, they have no cultural or ideological inhibitions against close association (unlike businessmen in a truly 'liberal' society, or doctors in a country having a deep tradition of individual practice, as in Britain); if their members do have largely identical, at any rate easily comparable, interests; if they are concentrated in small areas; if status considerations or the nature of the members' work lead to social as well as occupational identification among the members.[2] But here, as in everything else, art can guide and support nature.

The nature of the objectives sought by a group may also be a determinant of effectiveness, but chiefly because this factor affects the other internal group characteristics mentioned. I have in mind here primarily the difference between groups agitating for their own corporate interests and groups dedicated to social causes not necessarily arising out of their members' self-interest—'interest groups' as against 'promotional groups', as S. E. Finer calls them. The former generally have a more disciplined membership, more affluent treasuries, tighter bureaucratic organization, a more permanent and indeed also more active clientele. Their officers tend to acquire great skill in propaganda and negotiations, and they frequently have their own private channels of propaganda— journals and press departments, for example.

Policy. As there are many kinds of resources which constitute political capital, so there are many kinds of organizational forms and political skills which may be turned to account in the decision-making process;

---

[1] A fuller discussion of most of these points is given in Truman, *The Governmental Process*, part II, *passim*.

[2] Note, for example, the decisive role of the printers' high status among manual workers and of the peculiar nature of their work in producing solidarity and comradeship in the International Typographical Union. Lipset, et. al., *Trade Union Democracy*, 1957.

which is likely to exercise a decisive influence depends largely on the setting in which the group functions. Generals cut a wider swath in war or cold war than in peace; groups that want money spent have a relatively hard task in times of inflation and retrenchment. The pattern of policies enforced in a political system is an important determinant of the effectiveness of pressure groups simply because it is one of the situational elements which selects among the objective attributes of groups those which are of special political account. Take two examples. A policy may demand, in its formulation or administration, some skill or knowledge over which members of a special group have, or are believed to have, a monopoly; this is increasingly the case in the age of the social service state. Again, it may be impossible to carry out a policy without some sort of active support by the group; what use, for instance, is an agricultural policy without co-operative farmers? In either case, the pressure group concerned may not get exactly what it wants, but the need for knowledge and co-operation at least acts as a limit on what can be imposed upon it; usually, of course, the group's influence is much more positive than that.

Policy may also impinge upon the effectiveness of groups in another way: by affecting their size and the resources they command. When a group is subjected to public regulation and control its members are more likely to join organizations which press the group's interests. They are more likely to contribute to group treasuries; to tolerate specialization of leadership and administration in their organizations; to sublimate differences of interest and attitude for the sake of common ends, and to respond in a disciplined way to group decisions. Policy, in short, may make it easier to mobilize the potential power of groups by accelerating tendencies toward corporatization and by making for greater cohesiveness within the organized groups.[1]

[1] This is not to say that policy is the only factor affecting the corporatization and cohesiveness of interest groups. When different countries follow similar policies in regard to some interest, we often find the interest corporatized to a different extent and with a different degree of intensity; we may therefore suspect that deeper cultural factors also play an important role in determining what I have called the 'effective size' of interest groups. Take agriculture in Britain and the United States. Undoubtedly British control over agriculture under the Agriculture Acts is more intense than is the case in America, but the difference is hardly so great as to account, on the face of it, for the very large differences in farmers' organizations in the two countries. The British National Farmers' Union includes some 90 per cent of those eligible to join it and has almost a complete monopoly over agricultural group organization; in the United States there are three major groups and some minor ones, having a total membership of only some 30 per cent of those eligible. What can account for this, if not certain deep cultural attitudes toward organization? (See Beer, 'Group Representation', p. 134). However, *within* the two societies, that is, when other factors tend to be equal, one can trace the effects of policy on the corporate size and cohesiveness of pressure groups. Note, for example, the great growth of the American Farm

Governmental Structure. Finally, the effectiveness of pressure groups is also determined to some extent by governmental structure. There is, for example, a great difference between systems in which power is concentrated and those in which it is dispersed. In American government, groups can ordinarily get what they want, at any rate if they want something important, only by obtaining favourable decisions from a large number of bodies: legislatures, legislative committees, executive officers; this, as has been repeatedly pointed out, favours defensive pressure groups, those that want to maintain the *status quo*, by promoting delay and inaction as such.[1] But while under effective cabinet government it is much easier to obtain positive decisions at all levels, from Parliament to the lowliest interdepartmental committee, such systems inhibit many manipulative activities familiar in systems where power is widely dispersed (senatorial courtesy, for example) which give minor groups useful entrées into politics and means for getting 'positive' decisions.[2]

On a somewhat lower level of generalization, the influence of pressure groups may also be affected by electoral systems. Under proportional representation sheer weight of numbers is likely to be a matter of importance, while under the single-member system the distribution of members will be an important factor determining the 'effective size' of a group; a group the members of which are strategically posted in a large number of doubtful constituencies will be able to exercise influence disproportionate to its size in simple quantitative terms. So also will a group which derives special advantages from distributive anomalies in an electoral system; a case in point are American farmers, who are benefited not only by the over-representation of agricultural districts in the House of Representatives, but even more by the peculiar system used to elect the Senate. The National Farmers Union of England and Wales failed in its original aim to play a role like that of the American farm bloc in British politics, partly because of the existence of two highly disciplined

---

Bureau Federation as a result of agricultural policy during World War I, the depression and the World War II and post-war periods. (Truman, *Governmental Process*, pp. 90–92.) The impact of these policies has been greater on the Federation than the other two major farmers' organizations, the National Grange and the Farmers' Union, but this just because of the closer association between the Federation and government. In Britain, the growth of the NFU in response to the increasing involvement of government in farming is even more marked.

[1] See Truman, *Governmental Process*, p. 519 and Gabriel Almond, *The American People and Foreign Policy*, New York, 1950, pp. 144–45.

[2] These points are usually made to contrast cabinet systems and separation of power systems, but they apply equally to coalition *v.* single-party governments, i.e. unstable *v.* stable parliamentary systems. In regard to the opportunities it offers to pressure groups, both to gain access to decision-making bodies and to realize their objectives, French government is probably more like American than British government.

parties in Great Britain, but partly also because the British electoral system never favoured farmers as much as the American system.

Third, there is a relationship between the effectiveness of pressure groups and the character of the administrative structure upon which they act. A close 'clientele relationship' between group and administrative department always tends to give the group important advantages over others, if only by obtaining for it a permanent spokesman within the structure of government; it has been argued, for example, that in America the air lines have important political advantages over other public carriers because they have a public regulatory agency all to themselves (the Civil Aeronautics Board) while the other carriers all come under the jurisdiction of the Interstate Commerce Commission, within which there is consequently a stiff, often self-defeating, struggle for power. Much depends also on the power which a given administrative department can exert on behalf of its clients within the executive structure. Administrative systems are not merely tools for executing policy, but are themselves structures of power; they influence (often make) policy, and within them different departments carry different degrees of weight, depending on the political positions of their heads, the broadness and significance of their functions, and their traditions. In British government, there certainly is a world of difference between important departments like the Treasury, Supply, and the Board of Trade on one hand and Education and Pensions on the other. Whether a pressure group can carry great weight in government obviously depends on the power of the agency through which its weight is exerted, as indeed do also certain aspects of the form of its activities—for example, the extent to which its relations with government have the character of genuine negotiations; normally a President of the Board of Trade can negotiate far more easily than a Minister of Education, if to negotiate means to take decisions by bargaining with pressure groups. Finally, we should add to clientele relations between groups and departments, clientele relations between groups and legislative committees. Similar considerations apply, although the absence of specializing standing legislative committees make this point inapplicable to the country with which this case-study deals.

Summary

To sum up the argument in very general terms, pressure group politics in its various aspects is a function of three main variables: the pattern of policy, the structure of decision-making both in government and voluntary associations, and the attitudes—broadly speaking, the 'political culture'—of the society concerned. Each affects the form, the intensity and scope, and the effectiveness of pressure group politics, although in each case the significance of the variables differs—structure, for example, being especially important in determining the form of pressure group politics, policy especially important in determining its scope and intensity. Before any detailed discussion of the BMA's political activities I will sketch broadly, in light of these major variables, the conditions under which the Association acts as a pressure group.

II

The Setting of BMA Politics

The Framework of Policy

From the time of its founding (1832)[1] until well into the twentieth century, the British Medical Association played a part in politics only reluctantly. Its founders and early leaders thought of it as a purely scientific association; it was to bring medical practitioners together in local associations, to publish a national professional journal (the *British Medical Journal*), to sponsor research through grants or the formation of special committees, and to influence the profession in regard to professional ethics.[2] We may be sure that the Association's much professed dislike for political activity was genuine; some of the editors of the *Lancet* —next to the *British Medical Journal* the most widely read of British medical periodicals—carried on constant warfare with the BMA for its reluctance to enter into political disputes affecting the profession;[3] again and again, groups were formed by politically-minded doctors to step into the void left by the Association's studied political neutrality.[4] Political action, in effect, had at best a dubious legitimacy in the activities of the Association, due to the Association's image of its role; and this image, constructed out of attitudes concerning the proper functions of professional associations (perhaps also conceptions of the nature of politics), could be overcome only with difficulty. Nevertheless the inhibitions against politics were overcome, until today we do not think of the BMA as an organization for sponsoring scientific activities and fellowship among doctors but as the doctors' public relations office and trade union, its spokesman before the public and its collective

---

[1] The Provincial Medical and Surgical Association was formed in 1832; in 1856 it changed its name to the British Medical Association. Different works give one date or the other as the birth-date of the Association.

[2] E. M. Little, *The British Medical Association* (1932), *passim*, the centenary history of the BMA, is the source of much of the information in this part of the study.

[3] Particularly while Wakley edited the *Lancet;* see S. S. Sprigge, *The Life and Times of Thomas Wakley,* 1947 and S. E. Finer, *Life of Sir Edwin Chadwick,* 1952.

[4] To cite only one example, a large number of 'Medical Guilds' were formed throughout the country at the end of the nineteenth century, primarily for political purposes. See Little, *British Medical Association,* pp. 79–80.

bargaining agent with the government. This is not a misconception, despite the continued importance of the BMA's role as a scientific association. The Association's *Year Book* for 1956–57 lists fifty-seven areas in which important decisions were made by the various decision-making bodies of the BMA; of these thirty-seven were matters of politics and public administration.[1] A glance at earlier Year Books suggests, not surprisingly, that this growing preoccupation with affairs of government was chiefly a response to the increasing involvement of government in medical affairs,[2] although some of this involvement in turn (not much of it) was due to pressure by medical organizations.

The earliest political concern of the Association, as of most other professional groups, was to obtain legislation regulating entry into the profession. It could scarcely help being drawn into the agitation for the reform of medical practice during the 1830–1850s, the chief aim of which was to have the vast number of existing licensing authorities, universities and corporations, replaced by a single examining and licensing authority, enforcing uniform qualifications. Its first political committee, the Medical Reform Committee, was established primarily to press the Association's views on this issue; it remained in existence until 1858, when, with the establishment of the General Medical Council, the principal object of the reform movement was achieved.[3] It was succeeded by the Committee on Medical Legislation, which also

---

[1] BMA, *Year Book*, 1956–57, pp. 130–191.

[2] In 1904–05 only six matters were referred to the Medico-Political Committee of the Association. Its work required only six of the fourteen pages summarizing the work of the Association, two of the six being devoted to Contract Medical Practice, which was not a matter of public policy at all. (BMA *Year Book for* 1906, pp. 79–93.) Today it takes 40–50 pages in the annual report to summarize the BMA's medico-political concerns.

[3] The GMC was not itself given power to examine and license, but it was to supervise the standards of designated licensing authorities. Even today there are a great many of these authorities, including both universities and medical corporations, in Britain—a curious example, among many others, of how the ancient corporate organization of British society has persisted despite the broad rationalizing reforms of the nineteenth century. The General Medical Council has forty-seven members, including ten appointed by the medical corporations, eight by the Crown, eighteen by the universities, and eleven elected by the practitioners. In addition to its supervision of the training and licensing authorities, the GMC keeps the Medical Register and may expunge the names of unworthy doctors from it, a step tantamount to expulsion from the profession; punishable offences include felonies or misdemeanors, 'infamous conduct in any professional respect', but not the adoption of any theory of medicine or surgery. Being expunged from the Medical Register does not legally entail withdrawal of the right to practice, but registered doctors enjoy such enormous advantages over unregistered doctors that this point is a mere technicality; for example, only registered doctors may practise under the National Health Service, issue death certificates, possess dangerous drugs, etc. (See Carr-Saunders and Wilson, *The Professions*, OUP, 1933, pp. 83 ff., 110, 349 and 352, and *National Health Service Act*, 1946, 9 and 10 Geo. 6 C. 81, Section 79.

concerned itself chiefly with examining and licensing, in this case the battle for better medical representation on the General Medical Council and a Conjoint Examining Board. In 1903, a new committee with a much wider range of political interests, the Medico-Political Committee, was formed; this has now been succeeded by a large number of committees concerned with special aspects of medico-political policy.[1] The political affairs of the BMA have become too many for a single committee to handle.

The gradual broadening of the Association's range of political activities and the growing specialization of its political organs can be closely correlated with the development of public medical and sanitary policies. In the nineteenth century two aspects of these policies came to be of special significance to the Association: poor law medical practice and the conditions under which local Medical Officers of Health administered the growing volume of public sanitary legislation. Both of these areas of policy posed problems closely related to the organized profession's fight for a decent examining and licensing system. Under the Poor Law Amendment Act of 1834 medical services were provided to the indigent both at home, by District Medical Officers employed by local poor law authorities, and in a rudimentary hospital system which gradually developed in the Workhouses.[2] These services were supplied in the typical poor law spirit: grudgingly, and primarily with an eye on saving the taxpayer's money. Poor law doctors were prevented from prescribing expensive medicines; they were vastly overworked; they were generally appointed by competitive tender, appointments going to those willing to work for the lowest wages, a system which inevitably led to the appointment of unqualified practitioners, drunkards and ne'er-do-wells—those who had failed in the more comfortable, not to say more lucrative, forms of practice. The older and more august Royal Colleges, all companies of gentlemen and wits, were much too snobbish, and usually too uninterested in mere scientific standards, to bother about so sordid a business as Poor Law practice; hence it fell to the upstart BMA to fight the Poor Law authorities: to battle for better

[1] Little, *The British Medical Association*, p. 124, and BMA, *Year Book*, 1956–57, p. 13 ff.

[2] The Poor Law Amendment Act of 1834 made both administrative and substantive reforms in the old Elizabethan poor law. Under it, rudimentary domestic medical services—usually little more than indiscriminate doses of cheap 'physic'—were provided to indigent patients unable to quit their domiciles; a system of poor law infirmaries was gradually established after mid-century; and after a series of scandalous epidemics in the workhouses, primitive hygienic arrangements and medical care were introduced. (See E. L. Woodward, *The Age of Reform*, 1815–1870, Oxford, 1938, p. 430 ff.) From these primitive beginnings gradually evolved a very large public hospital service, incorporated under an Act of 1929 into the normal range of local government services.

remuneration, lighter workloads, adequate qualifications by Poor Law doctors, and their freedom from direct interference by Poor Law Guardians in matters of practice.

These activities on behalf of publicly employed doctors were not confined to the Poor Law. Along with medical services for the poor a network of sanitary services for all gradually came into being in the nineteenth century. An Act of 1848, passed under the impact of a serious cholera epidemic, created a central board of health and provided for the creation of local boards under certain conditions to survey and attempt to improve sanitary conditions. Again due to the persuasiveness of the cholera, an Act was passed in 1866 to put teeth into the earlier, predominantly administrative, legislation by laying down substantive standards for adequate sanitation.[1] The pivotal Public Health Act of 1875 further detailed and extended these standards; it was the first sanitary measure which was not a desperate reaction to epidemic but inspired by the good example of Birmingham, where, in three remarkable years, under Joseph Chamberlain's mayoralty, the town was 'parked, paved, assized, marketed, Gas-and Watered, and *improved*'.[2] There followed an important housing act (primarily concerned with sanitation) in 1909 and a good deal of progressive experimentation with more ambitious sanitary policies on the part of many local authorities. Like the poor law services, however, much of this legislation was vitiated by the indiscriminate hiring and sweating of public medical officers, many of them unqualified, most underpaid. The BMA spearheaded the fight against these conditions, its principal weapon being to refuse advertisements and to blacklist in its journal local authorities which did not conform to the standards it required—an effective weapon, since the *British Medical Journal* had, by the late nineteenth century, become the principal organ of communication in the profession.

Beginning early in the twentieth century innovations were made in public health policies which were bound to become of even greater concern to the profession. Sanitary services were greatly expanded, but, even more important, a larger range of medical services (that is, treatment) came to be provided by public authorities outside of the poor law, some to all members of society rather than to special classes. First came a network of maternity clinics; then, under the impact of the Boer War (when about half of the adult male population was found physically unfit for military service), the School Medical Service;[3] then Lloyd George's Insurance Act of 1911, which introduced compulsory national

[1] *Ibid.*, pp. 445–46.
[2] R. C. K. Ensor, *England, 1870–1914*, OUP, 1936, p. 127.
[3] The School Medical Service, created in 1906, provided for periodical medical inspection of school children and some treatment in special cases.

health insurance for all employed persons under a certain income limit[1] and abruptly made most of the doctors in Britain part-time public employees. After that came the Local Government Act of 1929 which permitted all local authorities to provide general hospitals and to take over Poor Law hospitals for general hospital purposes, thus gradually turning the bulk of British hospital services into publicly provided services. In the meantime, many special hospitals—infectious diseases hospitals, tuberculosis hospitals, mental hospitals—had already come to be provided almost exclusively by public authorities. Finally, we come to the climax of the whole development, the National Health Service Act of 1946, which 'socialized' almost the whole of British medicine.[2] Medicine, then, has become, in the course of a century or so, almost entirely a field of public employment, all the more so because of the expansion of governmental organizations, from police forces to the armed services, which use doctors; and medical institutions, with few exceptions, are now run by public boards and committees.[3]

This development of public sanitary and medical policies inevitably made the BMA more active in politics; but it has had other important effects on its role and power as a pressure group as well. First of all, it has engendered a constant growth in the Association's membership since mid-nineteenth century, when only a small proportion of practitioners were members. (See Table, p. 45.) The reasons for this growth in size, which can be correlated with the development of public medical policies, are plain. As medicine has become increasingly socialized doctors have been able to influence the conditions under which they practice only through corporatization, that is, through negotiations between governmental bodies and organizations formed by themselves. They have also come to realize that the power they wield in negotiations depends largely upon the strength and cohesion of their associations; at any rate, the BMA itself has made considerable capital of this consideration in its more and more intense membership drives. Gradually, therefore, the inclusiveness of the BMA

[1] For details of the Act, which is far too complicated to summarize in a note, see H. Levy, *National Health Insurance*, London, 1944, and the *Report of the Royal Commission on National Health Insurance*, 1926. Briefer accounts are available in PEP, *The British Health Services*, 1937, W. A. Robson (ed.), *Social Security*, Allen & Unwin, 1948, and H. Eckstein, *The English Health Service*, 1958.

[2] For the operation of the National Health Service, even more complicated than national health insurance, see J. S. Ross, *The National Health Service in Great Britain*, Oxford, 1952, and Eckstein, *The English Health Service*, among a host of other works.

[3] The only exceptions are some small and unimportant hospitals exempted from being taken over by the Ministry of Health under Section 6 of the National Health Service Act of 1946, chiefly 'nursing homes' (small private hospitals run for profit) and some denominational hospitals.

Table

BMA MEMBERSHIP[1]

Year	On Medical Register	Members	Per cent
1900	36,000	18,000	50
1910	40,000	22,000	55
1920	45,000	23,000	51
1930	55,000	36,000	65
1940	64,000	40,000	63
1950	80,000	62,000	77
1955	85,000	69,000	81

and its pre-eminence over other medical bodies have grown, until today it is by far the largest medical association in Britain, with a membership of over three-quarters of those eligible. It has become an indispensable provider of political services to the profession, and that, one may suppose, is the chief secret behind its success.

What I have called the 'effective size' of the Association has also grown under the impact of public policy. Along with an increase of members went an equally striking increase of wealth—at any rate in absolute terms, if not also in actual purchasing power.[2] Along with both went a still more striking development of internal bureaucracy: differentiation of functions within the organization, the growth of committees, and a much larger staff of permanent officials and clerks.[3] And much more money has been spent on publicity, not only in the *British Medical Journal* (whose supplement, devoted to affairs of the association and medico-political matters, has grown enormously), but also on a special public relations office and general relations with the public and press. Whether the discipline of the members—that is, their

[1] Source: *British Medical Journal*, 1950, I, Supp. 4 and 1956, II, Supp. 45.

[2] In 1904, the income of the Association was £51,000, of which £25,000 came from subscriptions. Fifty years later income was £273,000, of which £252,000 came from subscriptions. (See *Year Book*, 1906, p. 96, and *British Medical Journal*, 1955, I, Supp. 194.)

[3] Administrative expenses in 1904 were £11,000; in 1954, they were £106,000 (*Year Book* 1906 and *British Medical Journal, loc. cit.*). The Association had two permanent officials, the General Secretary and Medical Secretary, in 1904; there were sixteen in 1954: the Secretary, Deputy Secretary, Scottish Secretary, six Assistant Secretaries, an Assistant Scottish Secretary, the Director of the Empire Medical Bureau, the Public Relations Officer and his Senior Assistant, the Financial Comptroller, the Accountant, and the Librarian. This list does not include the nine doctors and eight laymen who constitute the staff of the *British Medical Journal, Family Doctor*, and *Abstracts of World Medicine;* these are also permanent officials of the BMA. Needless to say, clerical staffs have grown concomitantly. The Association had twelve committees in 1904, compared to thirty-five standing committees, six joint committees with other bodies, and fourteen specialized group committees in 1946. (See *Year Books*, relevant years.)

willingness to follow the lead of the Association's officers—has become tighter along with the growth of wealth, size and bureaucratization is much more doubtful; as we shall see, the Association's leaders have dismally failed to carry the members on some crucial occasions. But it is probably significant that there has been a growing tendency on the part of the government to make negotiations, even consultations, bipartite affairs between the Ministry of Health and the BMA, at least partly perhaps on the assumption that persuading the BMA usually is tantamount to persuading the medical profession.

Two other effects of the pattern of policy on the BMA's political position may be noted. One is that the Association has become indispensable to the government as a source of technical knowledge no less than as an agency of liaison with the profession. The administrative machinery of the National Health Service, for example, provides for professional advisory bodies on almost all levels; these bodies are designed partly to reconcile doctors to the Service by giving them a sense of participation in it and channels for the transmission of grievances, but they also provide important technical information to the laymen who administer all vital aspects of the Health Service. None of the Health Service advisory bodies are, on a statutory basis, BMA committees, but the BMA inevitably exerts a good deal of influence over most of them through the representation on them of BMA members; and many of these bodies, notably some of the Local Medical Committees which consult with the Executive Councils on the administration of general practitioner services, come close to being (in *fact*, not form) subsidiary bodies of the BMA.[1] Secondly, the Association has become important as an instru-

---

[1] Executive Councils administer general practitioner services of all sorts (medical, dental, pharmaceutical and optical) under the Health Service, in areas corresponding to the major local authorities, county councils and county borough councils (although they are bodies corporate which function independently of these authorities). In practice, their functions are primarily routine; they keep records of the lists of patients registered with doctors under their jurisdiction, transmit advice and instructions from the Ministry and other bodies concerned with the supervision of general practice, and pay doctors' earnings under the Service. In addition, however, they perform some discretionary functions of utmost importance to the profession. For example, they have some functions in regard to the distribution and placement of general medical practitioners. Control over distribution is exercised centrally by the Medical Practices Committee, which classifies areas in Britain according to the adequacy of the number of doctors, refuses admission (except in very unusual cases) to clearly 'over-doctored' areas, and decides among candidates applying for any given vacancy in general practice; many of its decisions, however, are taken on the advice of local bodies. The Executive Councils also perform important functions in regard to 'discipline', that is, enforcing contracts of service on general practitioners. General practitioners practise under the Service on the basis of certain minimal conditions: among others, that they keep adequate medical records, provide domiciliary services to patients registered with them, issue certificates required

ment for mobilizing the positive co-operation of the profession, without which public medical services obviously could not be provided at all. Positive co-operation in this case means not only willingness to practise under the National Health Service, but also willingness to serve on its administrative agencies, all of which make liberal use of medical person-

under the Insurance (and other) Acts, and provide emergency services to temporary patients. Complaints by patients that these conditions of service have been violated are almost all adjudicated on the level of the Executive Council, which may administer admonitions or levy fines on the practitioners concerned (the latter, however, only with the Ministry's approval).

In discharging these non-routine functions liberal use is made of advisory committees created by statute, the Local Medical Committees. The National Health Service Act provides that any committee recognized as representative of local practitioners may be designated by the Minister as the Local Medical Committee; in practice, and for obvious reasons, many of the Committees are organized by local divisions of the BMA, which treats them in its Year Books as among its own organs. This close relationship is underlined by the fact that the National Conference of Local Medical Committees is governed, and represented when not in session, by an Executive which is in fact considered a standing committee of the national organization of the BMA, and which includes the President of the BMA, the Chairman of the Council, the Treasurer and other BMA officers. (See below, pp. 62 ff.) It is, of course, important to distinguish here between relations on paper and actual relations. Formally, the LMCs and their National Conference are something different from the BMA and its branches. But when one comes down to the actual people involved and to actual channels of influence the paper distinctions tend to dissolve in the majority of cases. Only rarely does one hear of any antagonism between the LMCs and BMA bodies.

When problems regarding applications to practice in a certain area arise the Local Medical Committee is usually consulted and relied upon by the central Medical Practices Committee. Discipline is enforced on the local level by Medical Services Committees, composed of a Chairman and six members, three of whom are appointed directly by the Local Medical Committees.

Professional advisory committees also operate, on a non-statutory basis but nevertheless almost universally, in the hospital part of the Service and on the level of the Ministry, which is advised by the Central Health Services Council and its sub-committees. The CHSC includes the principal officers of the various professional associations, including the BMA, and a large number of other members (35) appointed by the Minister after consultation with these associations, consultations in which the BMA naturally plays a vital part. The Council has conducted extremely important investigations into technical aspects of the Service: for example, the feasibility and desirable organization of Health Centres, hospital administration, principles to govern prescribing by general practitioners under the Service, priorities to be awarded hospital patients in order to relieve pressure in hospitals, the care and treatment of elderly patients, the organization and processes of the Service in regard to the treatment of tuberculosis—among a host of other, chiefly more minor, matters. One may doubt whether the Service could function at all without a professional body to provide competent information and advise on matters such as these.

For greater details on the statutory provisions regarding Health Service bodies, see Charles Hill and John Woodcock, *The National Health Service*, London, 1949, and R. Ormrod, H. Walker, and J. H. Ellison, *The National Health Service*, London, 1950, reprinted from Butterworth's Annotated Legislation Service. For analyses, see Ross, *National Health Service in Great Britain* and Eckstein, *The English Health Service*, prev. cited, *passim*.

nel, some of which are composed entirely of practitioners, and a few of which could scarcely perform their functions at all without using professional representatives.[1]

The collectivization of medicine, in short, has led to the growing corporatization of the medical profession and given the medical corporations, especially the BMA, great powers, *vis-à-vis* the government. Because of the Association's opposition to many aspects of the socialized medical service proposed in 1944, and because of the public disputes it has sometimes had with the Ministry of Health since the Service came into being, the BMA is often thought of as the chief enemy of the Ministry, a victim of the policies which the latter carries out. Not so. In its present form as a vast, highly bureaucratized and wealthy organization it is the creature rather than the victim of public medical policies; and far from being involved in constant warfare with the Ministry it is engaged in constant co-operation with it—a highly useful adjunct to the Ministry's machinery of administration which, had it not already existed, the Ministry would have had to invent.

[1] On the central level of Health Service administration are two important, primarily medical, bodies. The Medical Practices Committee, the functions of which are discussed in the preceding note, consists of seven practitioners and two laymen. The Tribunal, which has jurisdiction in cases of serious malpractice under the Service envisaging the expulsion of the practitioner, consists of three members, one of whom must be chosen from a panel of practitioners for purposes of each adjudication. Practitioners also constitute a large part of the membership of Executive Councils and Services Committees (see previous note) and play an important role in the agencies which administer the hospital services. In the latter case, unlike that of the Executive Councils and central agencies, practitioners are not guaranteed a certain proportion of members on the agencies, but from a quarter to a third of the members of hospital boards and committees are in fact medical practitioners. One extremely important aspect of hospital administration is in practice performed entirely by professional bodies (and a good example of a function which could be performed by no other kind of agency): the appointment of specialists to hospital positions; this is done in all hospitals by the so called Appointment Committees.

While the BMA is not *directly* represented on these agencies, many of the professional representatives sitting on them are active in the BMA's national and local organizations and are nominated after consultations with the Association. When the Regional Hospital Boards were first constituted, for example, the BMA was asked by the Ministry to nominate professional representatives to sit on them. It provided a list of 85 names, of whom 27 were actually appointed. (*British Medical Journal*, 1947, II, Supp. 49.) Close consultations between the BMA and the Health Service agencies also take place, and on occasion they have made joint representations to the Ministry. (*British Medical Journal*, 1950, II, Supp. 100.) Some control, however indirect, is also exercised over professional representatives on the agencies, apart from initial consultations and nominations. In 1951, for example, the Annual Representative Meeting of the Association passed a resolution asking doctors not to serve on certain committees created by the Ministry without notifying BMA officials. A motion demanding official permission to serve on such committees was defeated, but it is clear that there is some indirect control—at any rate, that the BMA has attempted to exercise it. (*British Medical Journal*, 1951, I, Supp. 282–83.)

Structural Considerations
The General Setting. The structural setting of BMA politics is, in all important respects, typically British. On one side, there is a nearly monolithic formal organization of an interest group; a large majority of the eligibles are members of this formal organization; the organization is highly bureaucratic; and its officers enjoy a considerable amount of independent authority, that is, freedom from control of the rank and file. On the other side, the Ministry of Health enjoys a near-monopoly over the sort of decision-making in which the voluntary association is interested; it is, of course, also bureaucratically organized, in such a way indeed that most officials of the Association have opposite numbers in the Ministry with whom they usually deal. And between the Association and the Ministry there exists the closest imaginable clientele relationship. These generalizations are very large and need to be qualified;[1] but they convey the broad picture.

One important qualification which needs to be made is that, in comparison to the United States, there are an inordinately large number of medical organizations other than the general medical association in Great Britain. The BMA shares the field, in the first place, with the various royal colleges and societies: the Royal College of Physicians, the Royal College of Surgeons, the Royal College of Obstetricians and Gynaecologists, the Royal Medico-Psychological Association and the Royal Society of Medicine; these, to be sure, are chiefly academic and examining bodies, but not all of them are merely that; the members of the first three, in particular, although generally enrolled also in the BMA, tend to identify themselves as closely, perhaps more closely, with the Royal Colleges, and the Colleges sometimes play a role parallel to that of the BMA in politics; at any rate their leaders have influence sufficient to allow the Ministry sometimes to play them off against the BMA's leaders in difficult situations.[2]

[1] For example, the BMA has dealings with many departments other than the Ministry of Health. It deals also with the Ministry of Education (School Medical Service), the Ministry of Labour and National Service (Medical Inspectorate of the Factory Department), the Ministry of Pensions and National Insurance, the departments in charge of the armed services, the Home Office (e.g. on police matters) and the Treasury (e.g. fees for medical services provided for government departments by part-time medical practitioners). These, however, are relatively minor dealings compared with those the Association has with the Ministry of Health—save only perhaps for the Association's role in regard to practitioners in the armed services. This study, therefore, deals only with the relationships between the BMA and the Ministry of Health, especially in regard to the National Health Service.

[2] For example, when the BMA leaders were on the verge of inducing the profession to boycott the National Health Service prior to its coming into operation in 1948, it is supposed to have been the Presidents of the Royal Colleges, persuaded by certain important concessions by the Minister of Health to the specialists, who intervened to arrest the threatening rebellion. How could they

D

The BMA, in fact, tends to be, at core, a general practitioners' association; we can see this from any review of the members of its governing bodies and committees, its branches and divisions, as well as from the positions it tends to take in medical politics. Compare the following statistics, regarding the professional character of leadership

---

do this? By threatening to dissociate the specialists (that is, precisely those doctors with the greatest prestige) from any BMA action.

A few words explaining the Royal Colleges may be useful; their role in the profession is rarely understood. To grasp their nature, it is advisable, as with so many things British, to consider their histories. I shall only sketch that of the Royal College of Physicians. The College was founded in 1518 under a charter of Henry VIII, chiefly due to the influence of the revival of Greek medical learning in Italy. It was to be at once an academic body and a sort of guild, characteristics it has retained in varying forms ever since. An Act of 1522, confirming the letters patent granted in 1518, provided that no one should be 'suffered to exercise and practice physic but only those persons that be profound, sad and discreet, groundedly learned and deeply studied'. In practice this meant graduates of Oxford and Cambridge, or practitioners examined by the College. In addition, the College was given powers of general oversight of physicians ("to curb the audacity of those wicked men who shall profess medicine more for the sake of their avarice than from the assurance of any good conscience") and the right to examine medicines, i.e. to exercise guild functions. During its early history the College kept a close watch on medical qualifications, including those of Oxford and Cambridge graduates who were sometimes granted medical degrees rather carelessly; however, it stressed gentlemanly qualifications, general learning and social grace over purely scientific work (sometimes with absurd results) and, in the course of time, its characteristics as a guild came to predominate over its role as an academic examining body, in the sense that it became primarily concerned with the corporate interests of its members as against those of other medical bodies, a great abundance of which existed throughout England, e.g. the Company of Surgeons (also a sort of guild), the Society of Apothecaries, and the Barber-Surgeons Company. Its standards of examination, consequently, were extremely low. (See *Report of the Select Committee on Medical Education* 1834, parts i and ii, *passim*.) Under the Medical Act of 1858, passed in response to widespread agitation for the reform of the medical profession, the College became one of many bodies (eighteen universities, nine medical corporations) empowered to grant licenses to practise medicine under the broad supervision of the General Medical Council. It now gives examinations to anyone who has satisfied attendance requirements at approved places of instruction, grants licenses, and awards higher forms of membership (Members and Fellows) which depend upon higher academic qualifications and involve a more rigid code of ethics than the licentiate. To be a 'Member' one must pass an advanced examination; 'Fellows' are elected from any members who have become eminent in any sphere (not necessarily medicine). The higher ranks of the College consist primarily, therefore, of specialists, and only the Fellows have voting rights in the governing assembly of the College, the General Meeting. 'FRCPs,' of course, generally also have higher prestige and greater professional advantages than mere licentiates or members.

The history of the College indicates that it is something more than a mere examining body. It looks upon itself, together with its less ancient counterpart, the Royal College of Surgeons, as the high court of British medicine; nor has its aspect as a social fellowship, a corporation of gentlemen, wits and scholars, ever rubbed off entirely. The FRCP has snob-appeal; hence FRCPs are not merely, like Phi Beta Kappas in the United States, the members of a phantom fellowship.

For data on the Royal Colleges, see Carr-Saunders and Wilson, *The Professions*, Oxford, 1933, *passim*.

in the American Medical Association and the BMA. In the AMA specialists have a large majority of the official positions. Garceau found that of ten Presidents, three Treasurers and five Speakers of the House of Delegates whose histories he examined all were specialists, the majority professors of some branch of medicine. Among long-term committeemen he found specialists to have a 93·3 per cent to 6·7 per cent majority over GPs; among long-term members of the House they had a 71·4 per cent to 28·5 per cent majority; among short-term members a 51·8 per cent to 48·1 per cent majority.[1] In Britain these figures are almost reversed. Of the eight permanent officials in 1956–57 (that is, the Secretary of the Association, the Deputy Secretary, and six Assistant Secretaries) four had a background of general practice and four a background of specialized medicine. These officials are supposed to be merely 'executive' officials, but, as always in bureaucratic organizations, they play a crucially important role. Among the representative organs of the Association—the formal policy-making organs—the most important is the Council; of its elected members 38 were general practitioners, 22 specialists and 6 represented the public health services and armed forces' medical services. In local divisions and branches the preponderance of general practioners is even greater.[2]

There are also, we should note, a large number of lesser professional associations: among others, the British Post-Graduate Medical Federation, the College of General Practitioners, the Fellowship of Postgraduate Medicine, the Association of Industrial Medical Officers, the Faculty of Ophthalmologists, the Apothecaries Society, and the Society of Medical Officers of Health—although some of these are politically negligible. Finally, there is a medical trade union, the Medical Practitioners Union, and a medical affiliate of the Labour Party, the Socialist Medical Association.

There can be no doubt, however, about the pre-eminence of the BMA among these societies and associations, nor any about the growth of its

---

[1] Oliver Garceau, *The Political Life of the American Medical Association*, Harvard University Press, 1941, p. 57.

[2] Figures compiled from the BMA, *Year Book* 1956–57, and *Medical Directory*, 1957. They may be very slightly inaccurate, since often doctors do both general practice and some specialization, while others could be classified only tentatively on the basis of biographies furnished to the *Directory*. But the margin of error is probably insignificant. These figures suggest that Garceau was not on the right track in suggesting that specialists dominate large medical associations just because they have large incomes and considerable leisure for medical politics, and less to fear from the rivalry of substitutes than general practitioners (p. 54). Their political role in medical associations is not inherent in the character of medical practice but a reflection of national traditions and attitudes. Garceau's hypothesis that specialists dominate medical associations because of their greater talent and energy, their 'desire for prestige' (pp. 56–57), collapses under the same brute facts.

power relative to the other medical organization. This pre-eminence is not only the result of its size. It is also due to the fact that the Ministry has tended increasingly to make its negotiations bipartite discussions with the BMA, so that members of the profession have come more and more to think of the BMA as their sole bargaining instrument. Officers of the lesser associations do play a role in consultations and negotiations, but generally only a formal one—although sometimes, for tactical reasons (e.g. when BMA negotiators have proved inordinately stubborn) the Ministry has given them a significant part to play. For this tendency to make consultations essentially bipartite there are many reasons, obvious and not so obvious. The size of the BMA itself is clearly one. Historical reasons are another. During the days of National Health Insurance, for example, negotiations between the Ministry and the profession concerned general practice almost exclusively, matters in which important medical associations other than the BMA were relatively uninterested: when the National Health Service came into being, therefore, long consolidated channels of contact between the Ministry and profession already existed, chiefly through the BMA, into which business concerning the Service was quite naturally funnelled. Finally, the specialist organizations, especially the Royal Colleges, have always thought of themselves as scientific and, in a deeper sense, gentle-manly organizations, morally above the egocentric calculations of politics; even more than the BMA they have found it difficult to incorporate politicking into their range of legitimate activities. For this reason the BMA itself is now rather less a general practitioner's organiza-tion than in the past—at any rate, so the BMA itself has claimed. The National Health Service has drawn specialists willy-nilly into politics, but they appear to have looked less to specialists' associations to represent them than to the BMA or joint committees of the BMA and Royal Colleges.[1]

It is obviously a matter of great convenience for the Ministry to have available a single organization which can deal with it in the name of the whole medical profession; everything is simplified thereby, from the problems of the size of formal negotiating committees to the all-important matter of day-to-day contact and consultation between public and voluntary officials. However, what makes the Association such a convenient adjunct to the Ministry is not only its size and the identification with it of medical practitioners; equally important is its internal power structure, specifically the relatively great authority of its officers. When the Ministry's civil servants and the Association's officers and officials meet, they can generally make decisions binding,

---

[1] See, for example, *British Medical Journal*, 1948, II, 343.

for all practical purposes, on the parties for whom they speak.[1] In one sense this limits the power of both parties. The Association can rarely go to another part of the British governmental machinery to get what the Ministry denies or to prevent what the Ministry wants; the Ministry, in turn, can only rarely play off medical organizations or parts of the BMA against one another. But perhaps this is unimportant, since the power possessed by spokesmen of the Ministry and Association makes for particularly close relations between them, a tendency to keep others out of consultations, and a tendency to turn consultations into genuine negotiations. We cannot begin to grasp the nature of the proceedings between Ministry and Association, either their form or substance, without an understanding of these internal power factors. There are, of course, important limits on the power of the spokesmen on both sides, but they are no greater in one case than the other; indeed, there is, in all respects, a remarkable similarity between the distribution of power among the organs of British government and those of the BMA. This one might expect in a society having a deeply rooted political ethos—widely shared conceptions of the proper organization of power, public or private—and a highly distinctive style of administration.

Limitations on the Ministry's Powers. What precisely are the limitations on the powers of the Ministry of Health when it deals with the BMA? There is, first of all, the need to consider Parliament; but parliamentary questions and debates are no more (and no less) constricting a factor in this case than in others. As in other areas of policy, a core of MPs who take a special interest in medical and sanitary matters exists in both Houses, some of them doctors, others laymen with continuing interest in these subjects. Perhaps the fact that the chief area of activity of the Ministry, the National Health Service, is both a very popular measure and one under which many special grievances—the sort which give rise to parliamentary questions—arise, gives parliamentary proceedings on it special weight. On the other hand, the wide agreement on the principles of the Service has tended to shift conflict about it from the sort of general issues which generate parliamentary heat to technical matters of detail and isolated grievances which the Ministry is far better equipped to handle and in which MPs as a whole take little interest.[2]

---

[1] There are unimportant exceptions, as we shall see. But I am speaking here of what is normally the case.

[2] Almost any question period devoted to the National Health Service will bear this out. As illustration I have taken, at random, a session during which questions were asked (for oral answers) about the following matters:

1. Whether the Minister of Health is aware that doctors' lists in the London area of the Service contain some 8,000 more names than the total population of the area.

There remains one other limitation, more important in practice than parliamentary control, which arises from the administrative structure of the British Government. The Ministry of Health is not the only department concerned with the administration of sanitary and medical policies. Its policies constantly touch upon those of other Ministries and must be co-ordinated with them: capital expenditures on hospitals impinge upon the jurisdiction of the Ministry of Works, sanitation policies upon that of the Ministry of Housing, employment policies upon that of the Ministry of Labour; and over all the Ministry's activities involving the expenditure of money and bearing upon economic policy in the larger sense looms the omnipresent Treasury, the chief co-ordinating department, with its comprehensive powers over departmental budgets and its formal power to give or deny prior approval to a departmental project having a financial aspect.[1]

Closely related is the fact that the Ministry of Health is now a relatively minor department, having less weight than it used to have in the power structure among English departments—for example, on the level of the Cabinet, where the major interdepartmental disputes are decided. Until a few years ago it was one of the more powerful departments. The Ministry had jurisdiction not only over socialized medicine and environmental health services, but also over local government matters,

---

2. To what extent local health authorities (i.e. the county councils and county borough councils, which still have jurisdiction over environmental health services and, under the National Health Service, over a variety of services not strictly classifiable under exact hospital or general practitioner services: after-care, health visitors, home-helps, etc.) provide accommodation in their clinics for general practitioners for purposes of co-ordination.
3. What progress had been made, and was being contemplated, in the building of health centres.
4. How much heroin was in stock in hospitals.
5. Whether the Minister would relieve persons on low incomes other than those receiving National Assistance from having to pay prescription charges. (A nominal charge of 1s. per item on Health Service prescriptions is now levied as a revenue measure and to discourage over-prescribing.)
6. What action was being contemplated to facilitate the distribution of cod liver oil and orange juice to infants.
7. What progress was being made with suction limbs for amputees.
8. Whether the Minister will appoint a committee to inquire into the health of old people in homes administered by the local authorities.
9. In what areas there are shortages of doctors and auxiliary personnel.
10. Whether nurses' salaries are to be raised to keep pace with increases in the cost of nurses' accommodations.
None of the questions, except for number 3, raises any vital issue in which there is genuine general interest, however important such questions may be as a control over and prod upon administration. Questions for written answers deal of course with still more minor matters. (333 *H. C. Deb.* 1644 ff.)

[1] A detailed analysis of the Treasury's powers over other administrative departments in British government is given in S. H. Beer, *Treasury Control*, Oxford University Press, 1956.

housing, and town and country planning; it was one of the great multi-purpose departments, exerting considerable weight in the structure of Britain's plural executive, as is attested by the political stature of Ministers of Health, including Neville Chamberlain and Aneurin Bevan (both of whom, in a sense, made their careers at the Ministry). Ironically, it was the growing scope of public medical policy which led to the fall of the Ministry from the ranks of the great departments. The National Health Service simply gave it too much to do alongside its other functions; Aneurin Bevan held together most of the strands of its jurisdiction, but shortly after he quit the Ministry its non-medical and non-sanitary functions were given to a recently created department.[1] Subsequent Ministers of Health have either been less important figures when they took charge of the Ministry, or failed to use it as a springboard to higher things. The one possible exception is Iain MacLeod, the present Minister of Labour, and still a rising star; but MacLeod did not really make his reputation at the Ministry of Health. This is not to say that the Ministry is in any objective sense a negligible department. Any department which dispenses some £700 million per annum is bound to be able to make its weight felt, especially in preparations of the budget. But that it has lost caste since its halcyon days is indisputable.

The change in the power position of the Ministry within the structure of British administration has necessarily made some difference in its relationships with the BMA. Officials of the BMA now sometimes think nostalgically of the days when Bevan was Minister of Health, however much they may have abominated him during his long tenure

---

[1] Town and country planning functions were already being transferred from the Ministry of Health during the war, due to the fact that the Ministry was too busy with emergency medical problems to bother very much about anything else. In 1940 responsibility for planning the reconstruction of town and country after the war was given to the newly created Ministry of Works, although the Ministry of Health retained responsibility for town and country planning in general in its Town and Country Planning Division. In 1941 an inter-departmental committee was created to take care of co-ordination among Works, Health, and the Secretary of State for Scotland. In 1942, town and country planning functions were transferred to the Ministry of Works. At the same time, however, a Minister of Works who was enthusiastic about planning (Lord Reith) was replaced by one who actively disliked it (Lord Portal); hence, in 1943, a special Ministry of Town and Country Planning was created.

During and shortly after the war, the Ministry also began to share its responsibilities for housing with other departments (Works and Town and Country Planning). In January 1951, it was finally deprived of its responsibilities for housing and local government, these being transferred to a new multi-purpose Ministry of Local Government and Planning (a name changed later that year, in keeping with the Conservative Party's official distaste for planning, to Ministry of Housing and Local Government).

Details of these intricate changes are given in the Royal Institute of Public Administration's encylopaedic study, *The Organization of British Central Government*, 1914–1916 (ed. D. N. Chester, written by F. M. G. Willson), London, Allen & Unwin, 1957, pp. 162–8 and 176–80.

at the Ministry; for when Bevan was Minister, they say, the BMA knew that the profession had a powerful, if not always friendly, protagonist in the cabinet; they knew whom they had to convince (on all issues save matters of finance, over which the Treasury exerted its customary weight); officials on all levels of the Ministry dealt with their counterparts in the Association with greater assurance than they do now, knowing that their decisions would be subject to little revision at the cabinet and interdepartmental levels. As one of the BMA's senior officials put it to me: 'At least we knew then who our real enemy was; *nowadays negotiations are like shadow-boxing.*' This is important, if true, among other reasons because it makes negotiations as a government-group relationship more difficult.

However, I am not sure that this version of the matter is the best one available. Another interpretation may be made of the relative freedom of Ministry officials during Bevan's tenure which illustrates my point (though less directly) without making the same factual assumptions; and this interpretation may be more reasonable. According to this view, it was not Bevan's power in the Cabinet but his broad political interests and relatively slight interest in detailed administration in his own department which gave his officials such broad discretion in dealings with the BMA. Bevan was always heavily involved in party policy in the broadest sense and very active in party political propaganda; foreign policy and broad domestic economic policy seem always to have mattered more to him than the petty details of implementing a *fait accompli*. His successors, on the other hand (Marquand in particular), seem to have taken a more parochial view of their duties and tried to run the department more strictly than he did. Hence the atmosphere of shadow-boxing in actual negotiations, for the Minister, even when he takes a detailed interest in the affairs of the Ministry, rarely participates personally in negotiations.

This view has at least two things to be said for it. One is that Bevan was hardly so very powerful a person—in his own right, if not as the head of a great Ministry—when he was Minister of Health. In 1945, he was still something of an unknown quantity, not having held any political position, senior or junior, until that time. He was known chiefly as a promising nuisance on the extreme left wing of the party, and his closeness to Cripps, apart from his undoubted potential, was perhaps his main political stock in trade. It is an open secret that, throughout his tenure as a Minister, he was not in Attlee's inner circle and that the supplementary estimates he had to introduce during the first two years of the National Health Service lost him considerable face among his colleagues. We may doubt, therefore, the strength of his grip both on his own department and on his colleagues in the cabinet when matters pertaining to the Health Service were under consideration.[1] His ascent to the political heights is a more recent phenomenon; he really made his position in the party, first, by becoming a rebel, and second, by becoming a renegade to those who joined him in rebellion—a marvellous formula for success which Machiavelli somehow overlooked. In any case, the Bevan of today is not the Bevan of 1948–50.

Nor was his successor, Marquand, in any sense a negligible quantity. He had been one of only three new Labour MPs chosen in 1945 for ministerial office and was thought of very highly indeed. Although not a full member of the Cabinet, his office carried Cabinet status; that is, he was permitted to bring disputes before the Cabinet and attend any of its sessions, as a participating member, when matters under his jurisdiction were being debated. He also had a seat on the relevant Cabinet committee, the Lord President's Committee, which was the chief home policy committee of the Cabinet; and Cabinet committees nowadays appear to do far more important work than the Cabinet itself, particularly in regard to home policy.[2] But Marquand was certainly (departmentally, not personally) a man of narrower scope than Bevan. It is not just that his department's scope was more constricted, but that he seems to have taken a much narrower interest in it (as, it appears, did most of his Conservative successors). From this point of view, the crucial factor bearing on the discretion of departmental officials is not the power of the Minister as such but the degree of his involvement in extra-departmental politics.

Yet, these two factors are not independent of one another. When due allowances have been made for personal peculiarities, some scope remains for departmental conditions. The restricted scope of the re-organized Ministry of Health certainly has made it a less attractive place for men of broad political interests than it used to be. It tends also to restrain such men more than did the old Ministry, or perhaps attracts narrower men in the first place. It narrows the area in which they can make trouble and in which their co-operation must actively be sought by other Ministers. And it decreases the chances of Ministers of Health to be full-fledged Cabinet members and wield the influence which such a prestigious position still confers, even in this age of government by Cabinet committees. After all, a full member of the Cabinet can always

[1] This is, of course, a matter of interpretation on admittedly meagre evidence. W. J. M. Mackenzie and J. W. Grove (in *Central Administration in Britain*, London, 1957, p. 345) place Bevan in the 'clearly marked inner group of Ministers', alongside Bevin, Morrison, Cripps, Alexander and Dalton. I am suspicious of this list, for it omits Greenwood and Addison, and one wonders about Alexander's right to be included.

[2] See Beer and Ulam, *Patterns of Government*, p. 87–88.

make himself a nuisance to his colleagues; a Minister who merely has
'Cabinet status' can only do it on some occasions. The best interpretation, in my opinion, therefore is that changes in the position of departmental officials have been due both to changes in the 'objective' power
of the Ministry and in the way Ministers have defined their duties, but
that these two factors are themselves related.

Limitations on the BMA Leaders. What limitations circumscribe the
power of the BMA's leaders in their political dealings ? As in the case of
the Ministry, we must begin by examining the power of the Association's
representative organs. Do these in any sense significantly tie the hands
of the BMA spokesmen before the Ministry, preventing them, for
example, from entering into genuine negotiations ?

The counterparts of Parliament in the BMA, the bodies in which
'authority transcendent and absolute' is formally lodged, are a series of
annual mass meetings. The most important is the meeting of the Representative Body; this, according to the Association's Year Book, is 'the
governing body of the Association', composed predominantly of representatives of the local divisions and branches into which the BMA is
divided.[1] The annual meeting of the Representative Body lasts about
four days,[2] a fact which should itself suffice to make one disregard
the fictions regarding its authority. In point of fact, the Annual Representative Meeting does not resemble Parliament—the BMA does refer
to it as its Parliament—as much as it resembles the annual conferences
of the political parties. Like these conferences, it spends much of its
time hearing reports from the officers of the association; it debates,
perfunctorily, though often with heat, a host of resolutions and amendments submitted by the constituencies; it serves a useful function for the
leaders as a sounding-board of opinion in the profession; it is a gay
social and a solemn ceremonial occasion. That it will be nothing more
than this is guaranteed (not formally, of course, but in effect) by the
BMA's constitution, which provides that decisions of the Annual
Representative Meeting can rank as 'decisions of the Association' only
if carried by a majority of two-thirds. Needless to say, this rarely happens
against the opposition of the Association's leaders, and when it does

[1] The Division is the lowest administrative unit in the Association (although
some large Divisions are sub-divided into wards). It has local medico-political
functions and helps co-ordinate the work of Local Medical Committees and
local groups of specialists (e.g. Regional Consultants Committees), as well as
being a friendly and scientific society. Divisions are grouped into branches
which supervise and co-ordinate their work and act as 'constituencies' for
certain internal organizational purposes (e.g. electing certain members of the
BMA Council).

[2] On the request of BMA Council or a certain number of constituencies, special
meetings of the RB may be convened.

happen the leaders are often given ways out by the members.[1] The other mass meetings of the Association, the Conference of Honorary Secretaries of Divisions and Branches and the annual (and occasionally special) Conferences of Representatives of Local Medical Committees, are, in my opinion, of even lesser account. The first lasts only one day and is simply a friendly get-together of local and central officials—it is not even supposed to be a policy-making body. The second is the central organ of general practitioners serving on local National Health Service advisory committees.[2] Theoretically it can make decisions binding on the BMA[3] in negotiations concerning general practitioners; in fact, however, it generally confines itself to acclaiming *faits accomplis*, though, on occasion, it has attempted to exert considerable pressure on the profession's spokesmen. Essentially, the annual meetings and conferences are rallies: more useful in helping the leaders to put on a show of solidarity before the Ministry than effective in cramping their freedom of manoeuvre.

In recent years the Annual Representative Meeting has shown some signs of annoyance at having many of its decisions ignored by the Association's leaders and officials. Suspicion grew into vexation, vexation into a demand that the leaders account to the Representative Body on the disposition of its decisions. This probably has made the leaders somewhat more responsive, but they still tend to deal perfunctorily with inconvenient decisions, such as decisions which they feel would prejudice their position at the Ministry of Health; having two sides to contend with they could hardly do anything else. Resolutions passed by the Representative Body go automatically to the Ministry of Health, if they have a bearing on public policy; but, of course, not all are pressed with equal vigour and a flagrantly non-negotiable resolution may even be tacitly ignored by officials on both sides. By and large, the transmission of mass resolutions to the Ministry is a formality, and understood to be nothing more; what really counts is not the existence of a resolution but the extent to which it is urged by the BMA leaders.

The Constitution of the BMA tells us that its executive body is the Council, which is 'responsible for the management of the affairs of the

---

[1] In 1956 the ARM asked the Council to 'consider the desirability of abolishing the merit award scheme' for consultants. (*Brit. Med. J.*, 1956, II, Supp. 41.) In effect, judging from speeches at the ARM, this was an ambiguously worded recommendation to abolish the awards, but the ambiguous wording allowed the Council to oppose the recommendation and to carry the point at the ARM of 1957. For another example, where the majority was narrower, see *British Medical Journal*, 1949, II, Supp. 82.

[2] See note 1, p. 46.

[3] Actually, the General Medical Services Committee (the Executive of the Conference), not the BMA—but this is a paper distinction more than a real one. See below, pp. 62-64

Association'. Here we come much closer to the seat of true authority within the Association, although even the Council cannot be considered its real locus of effective power. For one thing, it is usually too large to transact business efficiently, having generally around 77 members.[1] For another, it meets only about seven times per year, for relatively short periods, which hardly suffices for managing the manifold affairs of the Association.

How precisely can we characterize its power? If the annual conferences of the political parties correspond most closely to the annual Representative Meeting of the Association, then the closest analogy to the position of the Council is perhaps that of the parliamentary parties, especially the parliamentary Conservative Party. Just as the parliamentary parties dominate the constituency organizations, so the Council towers over the ARM.[2] Just as the Leader of the Conservative Party is the locus of most of its powers, so the Chairman of the Council looms as the most powerful political figure in the BMA. He is elected by the Council 'for such time as it determines', but in practice, as in the case of the Conservative Leader, that seems to mean for as long as he wants to hold the office. The names of recent Chairmen—H. Guy Dain, E. A. Gregg, S. Wand—dominate the more important political affairs of the Association; the names of Council Members recur in the membership lists of the Association's committees, especially the more important committees; the Chairman is an *ex officio* member of all standing committees. Certainly the Chairman of the BMA's Council is, in practice, a

[1] The constitution provides that the Council may have 'not more than 77 members', but it usually has its full complement, or close to it. Members are chosen as follows:

a. 11 members *ex officio, viz.*: President, Immediate Past-President, President-Elect of the Association, Chairman and Deputy Chairman of the Representative Body, Chairman and Past Chairman of the Council (in the year following the year in which he ceased to be Chairman of the Council), Treasurer, Chairman of Central Consultants and Specialists Committee, Chairman of General Medical Services Committees, Chairman of Journal Committee.

b. 40 members elected by the members of the Branches in Great Britain and Northern Ireland grouped for the purpose.

c. 7 members similarly elected by the Branches not in Great Britain or Northern Ireland.

d. 2 members elected by Representatives of Constituencies in Scotland.

e. 1 member elected by Representatives of Constituencies in Wales, including Monmouthshire.

f. 10 members, elected at the ARM by the Representative Body as a whole.

g. 3 Service members, representing respectively the Medical Branch of the Royal Navy, the Army Medical Service, and the Medical Branch of the Royal Air Force, elected by the Representative Body as a whole.

h. 2 members elected by the Public Health Service members of the Association.

i. 1 woman member elected by the women members of the Association.

[2] See Beer and Ulam, *Patterns of Government*, pp. 146–153, for discussion of the power of the parliamentary parties compared to the constituency organizations.

far weightier figure than some of its formally more august officers, such as the President and Vice-Presidents of the Association and the Chairmen and Deputy Chairmen of the Representative Body; these are, in my assessment, predominantly ceremonial figures, comparable (with some notable exceptions, and stretching analogy pretty far) to the sovereign, the Lord Mayor of London, and similar figures in public politics—although the officers of the Representative Body play a more important role than the President and Vice-Presidents, especially through their *ex officio* membership on BMA committees.[1] In addition to the Chairman of the Council, certain of its members generally play an especially active and important role at the ARM, on the standing committees of the Association and in high-level negotiations. These we may compare roughly to the parliamentary executives—Cabinet and Shadow Cabinet—of the political parties, although the private myths of the Association demand that there shall be no formally organized Opposition to its leaders.[2]

Alongside these figures which loom large in the representative institutions of the Association we must rank, as usual, the Secretariat of the Association, the permanent officials who, like the higher civil service in government, supervise all the routine administrative work of the BMA and play a considerable role in policy-making as well. At the head of this bureaucratic apparatus is the Secretary of the Association; but so broad are his responsibilities (including, so to speak, ceremonial responsibilities) that the Deputy Secretary and the six Assistant Secretaries generally play a more active role in the political relations of the Association. Most of the day-to-day consultations and negotiations with political officials are carried on by these secretaries, or jointly by the secretaries and officers of the Association; moreover, there seem to be

[1] The Chairman of the Council is powerful, but, like the party leaders in Parliament, not a dictator. His power is conditional upon a certain 'constitutional discipline', requiring among other things that he shall not play a lone hand in the Association's public affairs. Usually, however, he is given a blank cheque, so to speak, to do whatever he thinks prudent by the Council members. In one case (Sir Henry Souttar) a *former* chairman resigned when he failed to carry the Council on a matter in which he had taken a personal initiative—Sir Henry was then President of the Association, a position not normally very powerful and only rarely occupied by former chairmen of the Council.

[2] The BMA does not have a formal cabinet and any attempt to draw up a list of the inner circle of very important Council members must necessarily be impressionistic. However, certain names loom considerably above the rest and should be included alongside that of the chairman Dr S. Wand, in an appraisal of the Association's structure of power. They include Drs H. Guy Dain (a former chairman of the Council and the grand old man of the Association), E. A. Gregg (also a former chairman), A. T. Rogers (formerly chairman of the General Medical Services Committee), F. Gray (the secretary of the London Medical Committee), and, below the first rank, such figures as Drs Cockshut, Davison, Jope, Knox and Davies. (These names pertain to the period covered by this study—up to 1955. They are based on personal impression, not on information from any outside source.)

exceptionally close relations between the members of the Secretariat and the more powerful representative officers—for example, between the Chairman of the Council and the Secretary and Deputy Secretary; such intimacy helps the Secretariat exercise a relatively free hand in relations with public officials.

In British government much important work is done by Committees, from powerful Cabinet Committees to ephemeral interdepartmental committees of lower-level members of the Administrative class; so also in the BMA.[1] Like the government, it is, to use Churchill's phrase, 'overrun by them'. Committees exist in the Association for almost every conceivable purpose. Standing committees run the gamut from a permanent committee for suggesting changes in the National Health Service Acts to a committee which manages the Association's film library; 'group committees' exist for almost every conceivable special field of medicine; *ad hoc* commitees appear and disappear with kaleidoscopic effect, just as in the organization of British government.[2] One should not, perhaps, put too much weight on these committees in the power structure of the Association. Most of them are in a sense themselves consultative bodies, gatherers of data and formulators of suggestions for the Secretariat and representative leaders; in any case, the more important committees are themselves effectively controlled by members of the Council and the Secretariat, the latter of whom serve as committee staff. The chairmen of the committees, the permanent officials and important Council members serving on them, rank among the power *élite* of the BMA, but the committees as such do not play a pivotal role.

Three Committees, however, do play a significant role in the public affairs of the Association, especially in regard to the National Health Service: the General Medical Services Committee, the Central Consultants and Specialists Committee and the Public Health Committee. These are worth describing not only for the important work they do but also because of the nebulous and illogical position they occupy in the structure of the BMA.

Formally, the GMSC and the CCSC (and their various subcommittees) are considered 'automonous bodies' within the BMA; in practice they control the more important trade union activities of the profession (such as salary negotiations); and between their formal

[1] See note 3, p. 45.
[2] *Ad hoc* committees are organized for specific purposes and cease to operate when they have discharged their functions. For example, a special committee was organized to prepare evidence for submission to the Spens Committee, formed in 1945 to make recommendations on the remuneration of practitioners in the National Health Service. In 1947, a special committee was organized to report to the Association on group practice and policy toward Health Centres. Most special committees, however, have more narrow and less controversial functions than these.

position and practical activity there is a significant connection. The General Medical Services Committee, in effect, represents all general practitioners serving under the National Health Service (not just those who belong to the BMA) and is formally recognized by the Ministry as their mouthpiece. It is responsible, in purely constitutional terms, to the Conference of Local Medical Committees, but that, as we have seen, is not a very important body; at the very least, in the words of one of its chairmen, the GMSC has 'an association with the BMA', and all attempts by members unhappy with this association to dissolve it have been summarily and easily put down.[1] Its meetings are held at BMA House and it reports to the BMA Council, which treats it without subterfuge as one of its own standing committees.[2] Why then the pretence that the Committee is 'autonomous'? *The British Medical Journal* has put it down to national characteristics; it would be more logical, concedes the *Journal*, to make the GMSC a BMA committee outright, but the British never carry logic too far. Still, there is some method in the madness; from certain standpoints, creating a paper relationship between the BMA and the GMSC would indeed carry logic 'too far'. The mythical autonomy of the GMSC is a useful pretence just because the BMA does not represent the whole medical profession, however large it may be, while the GMSC speaks formally for all the general practitioners in the Health Service; the myth therefore helps preserve the bipartite relations between Ministry and BMA. Moreover, the BMA still preserves some of its professional aversion to trade union activities, and sublimates it by pretending that when it is engaged in such activities it is not really the BMA; note, for example, the special creation of a phantom body, the British Medical Guild, to collect and administer strike funds in case the Association should ever advise a mass withdrawal from the National Health Service.[3] In the case of the Central

[1] See, for example, *British Medical Journal*, 1949, II, Supp. 204.

[2] In 1950, in debate on a resolution to make the relationship between the GMSC and the Council more 'definite', the Chairman of the Council asserted that the GMSC was already a BMA Committee and the chairman of the GMSC argued that the only thing missing was a formal paper relationship. (*British Medical Journal*, 1950, I, Supp. 119–20.)

[3] There were also legal and financial reasons for organizing a special phantom body ('a ghost of the BMA', as Lord Horder said) for this purpose in 1948. The BMA's articles of registration as a 'company not for profit' do not allow it to engage in activities which would make it a trade union or to collect or apply money for any purposes other than those specified in its articles of registration. Its lawyers consequently advised it that it could not engage in activities which would 'impose restrictive conditions' on medical practice (e.g. organizing a strike against the National Health Service) or collect 'fighting funds' for organized action. The alternatives were two. One was to make the BMA a trade union. Officially this was rejected because doctors, not standing legally in a 'masters and workmen relation' to the Minister of Health, would not be protected under the Trade Disputes Act; actually it was rejected clearly because trade union status was normatively repulsive to the Association's leaders. The other alternative was

Consultants and Specialists Committee there are even stronger reasons for clinging to the fiction of autonomy: certain important considerations regarding specialists' attitudes toward the BMA, which we shall touch on presently, and the simple fact that specialists are organized in a large variety of bodies outside of the BMA itself; in this connection we should note that while the GMSC speaks directly for general practitioners at the Ministry of Health, the Central Consultants and Specialists' Committee merely sends six members to another committee, the Joint Consultants' Committee (joint between the BMA, Royal Colleges and Scottish Corporations), which is recognized by the Minister as the mouthpiece of hospital medical staffs. The Public Health Committee undertakes medico-political activities for the Society of Medical Officers of Health (public health officers in the service of local authorities), which has even stronger normative inhibitions against trade union activities, and still stronger inhibitions against political activities, than the BMA. All three committees include a liberal number of BMA Council members who play, as usual, a vital role in their deliberations (most vital of all on the GMSC) and all are staffed by members of the Secretariat.[1]

---

to add the word 'Limited' to the title 'British Medical Association'; but that was also rejected, partly because it was thought to be indecorous to add such a frankly commercial term to the title of so pretentiously professional an association. *Ergo* the decision to establish a body parallel to the BMA for activities legally considered trade union activities. Who and what is the Guild? It is not open to membership (because then it could legally organize and help only the members), but simply a fund collected from various other medical 'defence funds' (e.g. those collected by the GMS Defence Fund, the Hospital Medical Staff's Defence Trust and the Public Health Service Trust): this fund is administered by a Board of Trustees consisting of members of the BMA Council.

For material on the British Medical Guild, see *British Medical Journal*, 1949, II, Supp. 31 and 1951, I, 230–31 and British Medical Guild, *The British Medical Guild: Its Nature and Purpose*, 1951.

[1] a. *The GMSC is constituted as follows:*
The President, Chairman of Representative Body, Chairman of Council, Treasurer, Chairman for the time being of the Conference of Representatives of Local Medical Committees (*ex officio*).
6 members appointed by the Representative Body.
33 practitioners elected on a territorial basis from among practitioners nominated by Local Medical Committees.
6 elected by the Annual Conference of Representatives of Local Medical Committees.
2 nominated by the Central Consultants and Specialists Committee.
1 nominated by the Medical Women's Federation.
1 nominated by the Public Health Committee in consultation with the Society of Medical Officers of Health.
2 nominated by the Medical Practitioners' Union. With power to co-opt.
It is constituted into various sub-committees (e.g. the Rural Practitioners' Committee). Only the two members of the MPU may be safely considered not to be BMA representatives.
b. *The CCSC is constituted as follows:*
The President, Chairman of Representative Body, Chairman of Council, Treasurer (*ex officio*).

Let us return to the point of all this descriptive detail. There exists in the BMA a body of leaders (both 'representative' and bureaucratic leaders) at least as powerful—exercising at least as much discretion—as the government officials with whom they deal. Like the latter, they function in a framework of publicity and control, consisting of the Annual Representative Meeting, the Council as a whole, and the Association's committees. This democratic framework, to carry the analogy still further, is supplemented by a free medical press (one much freer than in the United States); the *British Medical Journal*'s Supplement is freely open (or so it seems when one reads the letters it publishes) to the opposition, and there exists at least one large, extremely widely read medical journal, the *Lancet*, which is not the Association's organ and often takes an independent line. But this framework of limiting institutions leaves the leaders, both in theory and practice, wide scope of manoeuvre and generally condones (sometimes acclaims) even

---

4 members, being members of the Association engaged exclusively or predominantly in consultant or specialist practice appointed by the Representative body as follows:
  2 elected by representatives of constituencies in England and Wales; 1 by representatives of constituencies in Scotland.
2 members appointed by the Council.
32 members engaged in consultant or specialist practice, 2 being appointed by each Regional Consultants' and Specialists' Committee in England, Wales, and Northern Ireland.
10 members (or a lesser number) being persons engaged exclusively or predominantly in a consultant and specialist practice, appointed by the Central Consultants' and Specialists' Committee (Scotland).
5 members being persons engaged in consultant or specialist practice and partly in some other branch of medical practice.
1 by the Private Practice Committee.
2 by the General Medical Services Committee.
1 by the Public Health Services Committee.
1 by the Occupational Health Committee.
2 by the SHMO's Group.
2 by the Registrars Group.
1 by the Committee of each of the other special groups of members. With power to co-opt 3.
Also constituted into sub-committees.
c. *The Public Health Committee includes:*
The President, Chairman of Representative Body, Chairman of Council, Treasurer, two members of Council elected by Public Health Service members (*ex officio*).
5 members elected by the Representative Body.
5 members elected by the Council.
2 members nominated by the Society of Medical Officers of Health.
1 member appointed by the General Medical Services Committee.
1 member appointed by the Private Practice Committee.
1 member appointed by the Central Consultants and Specialists Committee.
1 member appointed by the Occupational Health Committee.
With power to co-opt 3 to secure representation of a particular class of experience not otherwise represented on the Committee.
Source: *Year Book*, 1956–57.

E

actions taken contrary to majority votes in the representative bodies. Freedom of manoeuvre is great, but limited, both on the side of the Ministry and the side of the Association; but it is limited less by constitutional myths and formal organizations than by objective elements in the relevant structures of power.[1]

We have described the limitations confining the officials of the Ministry of Health; what constrains the BMA's leaders in external relations ? Probably the chief limiting factor is a deep split in the British medical profession between general practitioners and specialists. That the BMA has been, and still is, predominantly a general practitioners' organization has been mentioned; so has the important fact that while a BMA committee speaks for general practitioners at the Ministry, a parallel BMA committee for specialists only sends representatives to another negotiating body. The split between GPs and specialists is due to deep historical and social reasons, apart from more obvious professional reasons (which operate also in societies where the division is less serious). In the early days of British medicine—before the reforms of mid-nineteenth century—a deep social gulf existed between the gentlemen-physicians (and the rather less respectable surgeons) and the forebears of the modern general practitioner, who were long regarded as mere artisans.[2] The BMA was formed, partly at least, to counteract the deep conservatism, social as well as scientific, of the members of the Royal Colleges in regard to medical organization and licensing. It was a provincial organization (note its original title, The Provincial Medical and Surgical Association), while the physicians' organization was predominantly metropolitan. These distinctions between gentlemen doctors and artisan doctors, liberally educated and technically educated men, provincials and Londoners, have long since ceased to have

---

[1] I have identified the great power of the BMA's leaders and officials primarily with the 'political culture' of Great Britain, but another explanation is possible which should at least be mentioned. It seems particularly difficult to achieve democratic structure in voluntary organizations (in any cultural context), and there are plenty of American groups which give their leaders as broad a range of power—broader in some cases—as does the BMA. (For examples see Key, *Politics, Parties and Pressure Groups*, p. 180 ff., and Truman, *The Governmental Process*, pp. 139 ff. For an analysis of the conditions of democracy in voluntary associations, see Lipset, et al., *Trade Union Democracy*, esp. Ch. 18.) Moreover, the power structure of the AMA, described by Oliver Garceau, in *The Political Life of the American Medical Association*, Ch. III, is not vastly different from that of the BMA described more cursorily here. I would suggest, however, that there are important differences in degree, in the extent to which actual power relations are sanctified by constitutional provisions (making it easier to maintain them), and in attitudes toward the exercise of independent initiative by group leaders, which are ultimately traceable to political 'culture'. These important nuances are obscured by analyses which follow too religiously the provocative and ground-breaking theory of the universality of oligarchy in Michels' *Political Parties : A Study of the Oligarchical Tendencies of Modern Democracy*, London, Jarrolds, 1915.

[2] See Carr-Saunders and Wilson, *The Professions*, pp. 75–76.

substantive significance, but the old connotations linger, supported by a general system of social stratification which discriminates with marvellous nicety among infinitesimal social differences.[1] Other differences reinforce those growing directly out of tradition. For example, consultants and specialists are, on the whole, far more radical in regard to public medical services than general practitioners.[2] Also, the special position of the higher consultants is symbolized by their refusal to engage in certain practices common in other parts of the medical profession and their subscription to a more rigid code of professional ethics; they do not, for example, practice in partnerships, or sue for fees in the courts,[3] and they have a particularly deep aversion to anything smacking of trade unionism: strikes and boycotts, for example.

The split between general practitioners and specialists is not, of course, the only division behind the façade of unity which the BMA usually tries to present. In any very large association, especially one approaching a monopolistic position, there are bound to be a multitude of rifts among members having different backgrounds, functions and interests. Within the BMA one can discern, for example, a good deal of tension between old and young, established and unestablished, practitioners. Unestablished doctors have even formed a sub-group *within* (but not *of*) the BMA, which studiously ignores it[4] and even treats it as a rival group; but they are represented on a sub-committee of the General Medical Services Committee (the Assistants and Young Practitioners Sub-Committee). For young specialists a formally recognized group of the BMA exists, the so-called Hospital Junior Staffs Group (formerly Registrars Group). Through these bodies young practitioners act as a sort of pressure group within the BMA, one having interests and attitudes significantly different from the more mature practitioners who inevitably control the higher positions of the Association. Young practitioners tend to be more 'progressive' in their attitudes toward medical organization than older practitioners,[5] particularly in their attitudes toward group practice and practice in Health Centres as opposed to the more traditional forms of individual practice which have persisted in the National Health Service.[6] They also have discernibly

[1] See, for example, the entertaining discussion in T. H. Pear, *English Social Differences, passim;* Allen & Unwin, 1955, see also note 2, p. 49.

[2] Evidence supporting this important point is given in H. Eckstein, 'The Politics of the British Medical Association', *Political Quarterly*, vol. XXVI, no. 4, p. 355 ff.

[3] This applies to Fellows of the Royal Colleges.

[4] See *Lancet*, 1952, I, 610–11.

[5] *Ibid.*, pp. 355–56.

[6] Although one of the special aims of the National Health Service was to displace individual practice gradually by various forms of group practice little has been done to achieve this. General practitioners practise under the Service very much as they practised before; the chief difference is that instead of charging

special vested interests, particularly if still unestablished, which clash
with those of older established practitioners. Under the National Health
Service, for example, a limit is placed upon the lists of patients registered
with general practitioners; it is obviously in the interests of young
practitioners to have this limit fixed as low as possible in order to create
greater opportunities for forming new practices, while the opposite is in
the economic interest of doctors already securely established.[1] An even
more explicit conflict of interests existed under the arrangements for the
remuneration of Health Service general practitioners made at the outset of
the Service, arrangements under which money for young doctors with
small lists was practically taken out of the pockets of established doctors.[2]

Still further divisions in the BMA exist between public health doctors
working in the local authorities' environmental services and doctors still
engaged in 'private' (that is, individual) practice; between the relatively
small number of trade-unionist doctors in the Medical Practitioners'
Union and the rest; between the even smaller number of socialist
doctors in the Socialist Medical Association and the predominantly
Conservative or neutral majority; between rural and urban practitioners;
and so on. None of these splits, however, is as deep or as politically significant as that between general practitioners and specialists; but for that
fundamental division in the Association's ranks we would hardly have to
justify our depiction of the BMA as a monolithic voluntary organization.

The result of its internal divisions is that the BMA, for all its mam-
moth membership, is often unable to speak for the profession as a
whole, and that the Ministry has a lever with which to counteract
drastic opposition (which Bevan at least seems to have used to good
advantage), not least because of the great professional prestige of the
leading specialists. There is in fact a good deal of tension in the Association between the general practitioner bodies (not only the GMSC but,
for all intents and purposes, the Annual Representative Meeting and the
Council too), and the Central Consultants and Specialists Committee.
Because the Central Consultants and Specialists Committee has to

private fees the government pays them capitation payments (so much per head
per year) for patients registered with them. See Eckstein, *The English Health
Service*, pp. 196–198.

[1] Originally, maximum numbers were fixed at 4,000 patients for individual
practitioners and 5,000 for those practising in partnerships where the average
number of patients per doctor did not exceed 4,000. See the *National Health
Service (General Medical and Pharmaceutical Services) Regulations*, 1948, SI,
1948, No. 506, s 13. These maxima were considered too high by the Ministry and
by young doctors finding it difficult to establish themselves; after a great deal of
negotiation with the more conservative leaders of the BMA they were reduced to
3,500 and 4,500 in an omnibus agreement on doctors' remuneration which gave
counter-concessions to the older doctors. A discussion of the negotiations is given
below, pp. 131–147.

[2] See below, pp. 126–130.

achieve unity with the other bodies represented on the Joint Committee for Specialists, it must insist on a certain freedom from the decisions of other BMA bodies; hence the BMA agrees to the separate representation of the Committee's views in case of internal disagreement. The occasion for such separate representations has not, to my knowledge, ever arisen, but not because there have been no disagreements; the reason is that disagreements have been ironed out within the Association for the sake of appearances. The fact is that some BMA members feel that the Central Consultants and Specialists Committee is practically 'out of control'; and on one occasion at least the tension between general practitioners and specialists came close to the breaking point.[1] The crisis never materialized, due to the usual internal accommodations. It matters tremendously to the BMA spokesmen that they be able to maintain the idea of the Association as a monolithic structure, if only for the purpose of offering a united front to the Ministry. Just for that reason, however, the positions which specialists in and out of the Association will take on medico-political matters are carefully considered by the BMA leaders and act as powerful restraints. We certainly have reason to think that many things the BMA has done, especially among its trade union activities, would have been done differently but for the influence, explicit and implicit, of the specialist organizations.

Some Relevant Attitudes

Despite the qualifications sketched above, the general picture I have given of the setting of BMA politics is accurate enough in outline: the BMA is a voluntary association impelled by the developing pattern of public policy, against some of its deepest corporative norms, to play an increasingly larger and more intense role in politics; it operates in a structural setting which encourages close relations, including much actual negotiation, between public and voluntary officials. For the latter fact, however, certain attitudes (other than attitudes on medical policy and constitutional practices) are responsible no less than structural factors. The tendency of Parliament to enact mere outlines of legislation nowadays, leaving to the Departments all the crucial details, frees the Ministry to negotiate where otherwise it would have no choice but to impose; practically every important section of the National Health Service Act, for example, calls for subordinate legislation, chiefly on points in which the BMA is most intensely interested (e.g. conditions of service). More important still is the very broad agreement on public medical policies in Britain today. The fact that the Ministry of Health

---

[1] On the occasion of the remuneration negotiations of 1955–56, when the BMA threatened a 'strike' against the National Health Service. 'Strike' here means the organization of mass resignations from the NHS, not withholding services from patients.

is now a rather weak department is important to an understanding of BMA politics, but it is not crucial, for most of the matters on which the BMA and Ministry consult pose relatively minute, chiefly technical, problems, in which the Ministry has a relatively free hand. The power structure of the plural executive comes into play only in case of major issues, such as conflicts over remuneration, which have important political, financial, or administrative implications; but a broad consensus on policy clearly minimizes such issues. Consensus also augments the power of the leaders of the BMA, partly by minimizing tensions among the wings of the Association, partly by making more docile the Association's representative bodies. Broad agreement on medical policy thus frees both sides from pressures normal in more controversial areas of policy, while at the same time it brings the Ministry's and BMA's officials closer together, as does any fundamental agreement among men.

This is the broad picture; yet we cannot quite grasp what happens when BMA and government spokesmen come face to face without taking into account certain other attitudes as well. For example, in evaluating the effectiveness of the BMA in politics it is important to be aware of the self-effacing attitudes laymen generally assume when confronted by professionals, especially professionals who practise a calling invested by popular attitudes with such high prestige and deep mystery as medicine. It is not only British corporatism which demands that the Ministry seek BMA approval for its policies, whether they touch upon the clinical relationship or not, but also the public belief (not, I think, entirely warranted) that doctors always know best what is good for the organization of medicine. The BMA certainly commands technical knowledge which the Ministry can ill afford to ignore; but equally important are public myths about the scope of its expertise and ill-defined fears regarding the tensions and fragile balances of the doctor-patient relationship. The BMA need only raise the spectre of interference in the clinical practice of medicine to mobilize a good deal of opinion on its side. Such attitudes give it a specially powerful position *vis-à-vis* public officials, compared to other pressure groups.

The internal norms of the Association, however, tend to reduce these advantages somewhat. The taboo on overt politics, for example, prevents any close identification with a political party. Even discounting the countervailing power of the specialists and the lingering distaste for trade union activity at BMA Headquarters, certain activities, such as strikes and boycotts against the socialized medical services, are, at best, remote possibilities, for the Hippocratic tradition make it normatively difficult for doctors to withhold services from patients, even where paper arrangements for the supply of services are made to satisfy the literal code of professional ethics. Nor would professional norms allow the

Association to engage in the more blatant kinds of public propaganda, even if there were reasons to do so. The BMA, which contents itself with an efficient but restrained Public Relations Officer, is far more inhibited in this respect than the AMA, which has made liberal use of Madison Avenue techniques. 'Internal propaganda' is somewhat more effective but also restrained by important taboos. The *British Medical Journal* provides a useful platform for the oligarchy, and its 'leaders' (editorials) almost invariably express official attitudes. Quite apart, however, from the availability of the *Lancet* as a medium for non-official views, the *Journal*'s Supplement (its principal organ for views on the Association's political affairs)[1] serves as an open forum for the rank and file. It seems to be conducted with scrupulous regard for the rights of dissident groups; this the English conception of authority, for all its toleration of independent leadership, demands. The correspondence columns, for example, while giving most space to doctors supporting the oligarchy, do give a good deal of space to rebels, enough at any rate to give one a clear idea of the range of non-official views in the profession. In this respect too, the BMA seems more restrained than the AMA.[2]

Finally, the dominant attitudes of the profession toward the Association must also be listed largely on the debit side (although in certain circumstances, as we have seen, they belong on the credit side). Not only do specialists tend to dissociate themselves from the Association, but the membership as a whole is perfunctory rather than active. Truman maintains that the strength of groups is determined by the frequency and persistence of 'interactions' among its members. Now there is in the BMA, both on the national and local levels, a small group of activists—medical politicians, as it were—who 'interact' frequently as members of the Association and identify themselves intensely with it, but this group is small indeed. For most doctors membership in the BMA amounts to little more than buying the *Journal*, just as most members of the Automobile Association are in it merely to obtain certain services. Most doctors do not attend branch meetings, or participate in the drafting of resolutions or the election of delegates to the Representative Body, or organize local fighting funds. Hence their loyalties to the BMA are bound to be rather weak.[3] This is not unusual:

[1] Note, incidentally, that political news, including news about internal politics, is generally excluded from the principal pages of the *Journal*—a reflection of the inhibitions against politics in what purports to be primarily a scientific association. Only the most vital political issues concerning the profession are dignified by editorials in the *Journal* itself.

[2] See Garceau, *Political Life of the American Medical Association*, p. 96 ff., and Truman, *The Governmental Process*, pp. 196–97.

[3] We should, however, bear in mind an important qualification of this argument. Truman's theory is that the strength of a group is determined not only by the frequency and persistence of interaction among its members, but also by the

all groups are composed of activists who run the groups' affairs and a largely apathetic rank and file, especially large voluntary associations; *ergo* (among other reasons) the iron law of oligarchy. However, there are differences in degree of apathy among organizations, and in the medical profession apathy happens to be very high, perhaps inevitably so. Medicine is a lonely and time-consuming craft. It does not ordinarily give the practitioner much time for 'interacting' with anyone but his patients; nor does it encourage corporate habits. Only the members of hospital 'teams' really function collectively on the job; for others, medical practice is a very private craft, whatever formal partnership arrangements a doctor may engage in. In many cases, of course, the resulting lack of interest and participation in corporate affairs is an asset to the BMA: it gives the leaders and officials great power to commit the Association and practically rules out the mobilization of an opposition which might split it on important occasions. On the other hand, in the case of very important disputes with the Ministry, when the task of the leaders is not to prevent open opposition but to mobilize the membership for concerted action (e.g. 'strikes'), their work is often nullified by the indifference of the rank and file; indifference, in this case, reinforces powerful ethical considerations. There is power which rests on sympathy and power which rests on apathy; that of the BMA's leaders rests mainly on apathy. It is therefore easily turned into weakness under circumstances requiring strong corporate cohesion.[1]

Whether and how these attitudes tending to extend or limit the BMA's power come into play also depends on circumstances. The attitudes I have sketched should not be thought of as forces that tend to cancel one another in all cases, but as forces that are evoked with different degrees of intensity by different issues. If, for example, an issue poses important technical problems, attitudes enhancing the Association's power are evoked; if it is a trade union matter, requiring a show of professional force, negative attitudes play a more important role. We shall see this more concretely in the chapter on the political effectiveness of the BMA (Chapter IV).

---

extent to which members have overlapping affiliations with other groups (pp. 157–67). The factors which prevent intense participation by doctors in BMA affairs also prevent intense participation in other groups. Doctors are notoriously bad joiners; while their identification with the BMA tends to be rather low, other affiliations are rarely more intimate, which prevents important conflicts of loyalty. Apathy towards the BMA therefore works, *ordinarily*, in the BMA leaders' favour, simply because of the lack of strong sympathies in the profession for other groups and associations. This qualification even applies to conflicts between general practitioners and specialists. More often than not specialists hold their views with such lack of intensity that they cannot be a very effective counterpoise to official BMA policy, except as a latent threat and in unusual circumstances.

[1] See page 69.

III

Channels of Influence

Non-Departmental Channels: Electorate, Parties and Parliament

What are the actual relationships between the BMA and the government? Broadly speaking, pressure groups may try to exert political influence through four major channels: the electorate, the political parties, the legislature and the administrative departments. That British pressure groups tend to concentrate on the last of these channels is borne out by the BMA. The Association does try to influence opinion through other channels as well, but these are mere adjuncts to its primary relationship with the Ministry of Health, not only because of the power position of the Ministry but also because of certain normative inhibitions on the part of the Association and other attitudes affecting its political position which will presently be described. Nevertheless, we cannot ignore its non-departmental channels of influence entirely.

It goes without saying that the BMA tries to persuade public opinion to its point of view, but it does not try to do so very intensely. Nor do its leaders and officers seem to take public opinion very seriously as a power factor in their pressure group activities. Since the war the Association has acquired a Public Relations Department, headed by a journalist with considerable experience,[1] and a public relations consultant to advise it in 'getting its views across to the public'; most of the Divisions also have at least a rudimentary public relations organization.[2] The Association arranges occasional public lectures and press conferences; the Annual Representative Meeting is open to the press; the Public Relations Department prints leaflets and posters, and acts as an information bureau for journalists.[3] But much more could be done along these lines than the BMA does. For example, leaflets are distributed only to practitioners rather than on a broader national scale; BMA posters rarely, if ever, appear in public places; and the Public Relations Office is very small. At present it consists of the Public Relations Officer, his Senior Assistant, two private secretaries and three clerical assistants. The BMA spent on

---

[1] The present Public Relations Officer came to the Association from the BBC, having previously been with the *Manchester Gaurdian;* his assistant also has had experience in broadcasting.

[2] *British Medical Journal*, 1946, I, Supp. 53.

[3] *Ibid.*, 1949, II, Supp. 135.

it £13,750 out of a total budget (in 1957) of £295,582 (4·6 per cent).

Publicity is used chiefly as a tactical weapon for nudging the Ministry into certain positions or whipping up a show of unity in the profession. A good example of its use for both purposes occurred in 1943. The Beveridge Report on social security had been published in 1942, including a recommendation for a comprehensive national health service which the medical profession had accepted, at least in principle. Negotiations between representatives of the BMA and the Ministry of Health on the concrete shape the service was to take were begun almost immediately; for the sake of free communication and a constructive exchange of views, these discussions were supposed to be secret. But having accepted socialized medicine in principle the Association became panic-stricken over details, especially the possibility of a full-time salaried service of practitioners; accordingly its aim became the postponement of action, even of planning for action, for as long as possible. To achieve this end, it broke the secrecy of the negotiations with a series of public mass-meetings, following a still unexplained leak to the popular press on certain aspects of the discussions. The aim was not, however, to condition public opinion against socialized medicine; it was to nip in the bud any thoughts of salaried service under the proposed scheme with a show of mass indignation, and to transfer the consultations from the privacy of the Ministry, where they could proceed swiftly and efficiently, to the public limelight—the BMA suggested a Royal Commission—where they always proceed more sluggishly.[1]

Publicity is rarely used for any broader strategic purpose by the Association. For this, professional inhibitions against any sort of vulgarity are partly responsible, but only partly. Equally important is the fact that the audience for medico-political issues is ordinarily very limited. The BMA and its political affairs simply are not very newsworthy, and this in turn can be explained by the absence of any important disagreements on medical policy in Britain. Even during the tense days between the coalition government's publication of its White Paper on the National Health Service (in 1944) and the passage of the Labour government's National Health Service Act (in 1946) there was no question of any fundamental disgreement. The issues which agitated the profession were matters of detail—administrative organization and conditions of service—and in these little public interest could be sustained. What was the case then is true with a vengeance now, for even matters of administrative organization and conditions of service have now mainly been shifted to the large reservoir of British consensus, and most issues which arise between the Ministry and the Association are matters in which even doctors rarely take a sustained

[1] Eckstein, *The English Health Service*, Ch. 5 and 6.

interest. In individual grievances arising under the Service—maltreated patients, doctors dismissed from positions, doctors punished for violating their contracts of service—there is a great deal of interest, to be sure, but this is something different from interest in genuine issues; it is little more than a special facet of the universal appetite for scandal.

The strict insistence of the Association on party-political neutrality also tends to inhibit its use of publicity as an important political weapon, for the BMA does not like to antagonize any of the political parties by converting departmental into political issues. It follows that it also steers studiously clear of any identification with a political party. When Dr Charles Hill (an official of the BMA since 1932, its Secretary since 1944, and, because of his radio talks as the 'Radio Doctor' during the war, the most famous practitioner in Britain) was elected to Parliament in 1950, a very considerable stir arose in the correspondence columns of the *British Medical Journal* because Hill had not immediately resigned his secretaryship. It is doubful whether Hill had seriously considered hanging on to his position in the Association in the first place, but the fuss created by his election is noteworthy because it brought to the surface the deep inhibitions throughout the profession against overt political action or political identifications. In any case, Hill resigned later in 1950.[1] The political parties themselves, of course, have little reason to seek any closer identification with the BMA than the BMA wants with them, for doctors are neither a very sizeable nor a very strategically placed electorate.

Finally, the BMA wages few publicity campaigns simply because it seldom has any pressing need to wage them. American pressure groups, as S. E. Finer has pointed out,[2] tend to make much more use of publicity than English pressure groups because they can obtain positive decisions only by persuading a large number of organs of government, something which can be done best by mobilizing public opinion on a grand scale. This, of course, is an over-generalization. Some British pressure groups do use public agitation, but almost always for exceptional reasons. They may have no reliable spokesmen in the machinery of government, or they may want decisions which cut across many jurisdictions or touch on matters of high policy (including important financial policy).[3] In the Ministry of Health, the BMA does have a reliable, and usually friendly,

[1] *British Medical Journal*, 1950, II, 1107. Stewart suggests that Hill resigned because of the pressure of parliamentary business. (*British Pressure Groups*, p. 153.) The events leading up to his resignation suggest that Stewart is wrong.

[2] S. E. Finer, *Anonymous Empire*, pp. 92–93.

[3] A good case in point is the Equal Pay Campaign Committee; see Allen Potter, 'The Equal Pay Campaign Committee: A Case-Study of a Pressure Group', *Political Studies*, February 1957. Another is the Roads Campaign Council; see S. E. Finer, 'Transport Interests and the Roads Lobby', *Pol. Quarterly*, vol. 29, no. 1.

mouthpiece; few of the decisions it wants ever cut across other jurisdictions; and, except for money, its purposes rarely reach the level of
high policy. Therefore, it wisely eschews costly and politically com-
promising attempts to stir up the public.

Because of its careful avoidance of party alignments the BMA is
represented in Parliament only in so far as certain MPs are doctors and
willing to act as the Association's spokesmen; still, its parliamentary
activities are rather more important than its efforts to mobilize public
opinion. It employs a Parliamentary Agent (that is, a legal firm specializing in legislative business) to scrutinize legislation and notify it of
anything relevant.[1] The chief function of the public relations consultant
mentioned above is to bring together BMA officers and Members of
Parliament (or other notables); he receives a substantial honorarium for
making available his wide connections, in effect for serving as a social
intermediary. Unlike many other British pressure groups, the BMA—
probably because of its reluctance to identify with party politicians—
does not 'retain' any MPs (that is, pay them salaries or help them to
meet election expenses, practices which are both legal and widespread
in Britain), but there are a large number of 'interested MPs' to represent
it in both Houses of Parliament.[2] At present, ten MPs are medical men[3]
and there are also a small number of medical peers; through these the
Association always manages to raise parliamentary questions it wants

[1] Constant vigilance is kept over even the most minor parliamentary transactions affecting medical practice. In 1946, for example, the Southend Corporation
promoted a private bill empowering the Medical Officer of Health to obtain
warrants to enter premises where notifiable disease is suspected. Representatives
of the BMA approached the promoters in order to have a clause introduced
prohibiting the examination of patients by Medical Officers of Health where the
patient was already under the treatment of another practitioner, in accordance
with the strictures of professional ethics on simultaneous treatment by numerous
doctors. (*British Medical Journal*, 1947, I, Supp. 32.) This is quite normal
operating procedure for British associations, for their interests can be seriously
prejudiced by private legislation if they are not constantly on the lookout. (For
the nature of private bill legislation, see Jennings, *Parliament*, 2nd ed., 1957,
ch. 13.) The main function of parliamentary agents has been to keep an eye on
such bills; they are not, consequently, to be thought of as firms of professional
lobbyists, although recently there has been a tendency for the agents to act as
lobbyists or public relations agencies. (See the *Joint Report of the House of Lords
and the House of Commons on the Procedure of Private Bills*, HC 139-1, 1955.)
The BMA's parliamentary agents examine both public and private bills.

[2] However, the BMA did establish a Medical Representation in Parliament
Fund in 1919, to assist candidates likely to express the Association's views. This
fund got little support from the profession and had to be wound up. After the
elections of 1945 another representation fund was created, to be administered by
the Parliamentary Elections Committee of the BMA. It received equally bad
support, despite the urgent political issues then before the profession. This fund
still seems to be in existence, but proceeds from it have seldom been used. See
also Stewart, *British Pressure Groups*, pp. 171–72.

[3] S. E. Finer, *Anonymous Empire*, 1958, p. 135. 'Medical men' includes doctors,
surgeons, and dentists.

answered, or to press for debates it wants held. In addition, Parliament contains a number of non-medical MPs with a continuing interest in medical affairs and close connections in medical organizations who may also be considered 'interested MPs'.[1] The medical MPs and peers are organized in a non-partisan Parliamentary Medical Group (which also includes some non-medical MPs),[2] and this group has close relations with the BMA (although it has not always unreservedly supported the Association, due in part to the dominant role of Socialist doctors in its councils).[3] Apart from acting through them, the Association also circularizes MPs as a whole on important matters. Finally, we must list among its parliamentary channels of influence personal acquaintances and friendships between certain BMA officials and important MPs; in BMA—Government relations, as in all British life, the 'old boy network' plays an important role, although there can be no question of any dubious intriguing through such informal personal contacts.

Collusion between MPs and BMA officials would in any case be of little use, due to the limited powers of Parliament in the British structure of decision-making. Nevertheless, the fact that the BMA seeks at least some influence in Parliament suggests that Parliament does play some sort of positive role in medico-political matters. This role is not restricted to venting grievances and publicizing medico-political points of view; it also involves real participation in policy-making. For example, some years ago Parliament managed to have withdrawn an announced governmental policy strongly opposed by the BMA. The Government had decided to ban the manufacture of heroin, but the BMA was able to drum up great back-bench support in both parties against the decision; the *coup de grâce* was delivered by Lord Jowitt, the former Lord Chancellor, who raised such complicated legal objections in the House of Lords debate on the matter that the Government, beset both by its opponents and supporters, felt compelled to withdraw the ban.

But this is very unusual, and the fact that such a minor incident could become in any sense notorious is itself significant. Not only does Parliament rarely play so decisive a role in British governmental decision-making, but the subjects of medical politics rarely stir parliamentary

[1] An example is Sir Frederick Messer, a Labour member, who is hardly a spokesman for the BMA but not infrequently on its side (for example, in the Registrar dispute; see below, pp. 118). Sir Frederick has been Chairman of the Central Health Services Council, a member of the Ministry of Education Advisory Committee on Handicapped Children, Vice-President of the Medical Superintendents Society, and Chairman of the Industrial Orthopaedic Society, among many other similar positions. Another example is Sir Hugh Nicholas Linstead, a Conservative MP since 1942 and the Secretary of the Pharmaceutical Society of Great Britain since 1926, who is even more frequently on the side of the BMA when medico-political issues arise in Parliament.

[2] Stewart, *British Pressure Groups*, p. 162.

[3] Eight of the ten medical MPs are in the Labour Party.

interest much more than public interest. It is significant that the Parliamentary Medical Committee has long been restive under what it considers neglect by BMA headquarters. The medical MPs and their friends have wanted to be used as the primary channel of political influence by the BMA: as agents of negotiation and consultation, for example. The BMA has never dreamed of giving them such an important role to play in medical politics, not only because the Committee includes too many 'unreliable' practitioners (and men regarded as amateurs and interlopers by the BMA bureaucrats), nor because medical MPs are identified with political parties, but because neither Parliament, nor the electorate, nor the parties, are the main arena of medical politics.

Departmental Channels: Relations with the Ministry of Health

Medical politics in Britain consist chiefly of relations between the Ministry of Health and the BMA's leaders and officials—a closed network of relations into which other parties (the Treasury, the Cabinet, the Royal Colleges, public opinion in the medical profession as a whole) only occasionally intrude. I shall describe this network of relations under three headings: its scope (the range of subjects on which the Ministry and Association consult or negotiate), its structure (the machinery of consultation and negotiations), and its 'spirit' (the attitudes of the two parties toward one another).

Scope. It is an understatement to say that the range of subjects on which the Ministry of Health deals with the BMA is very broad. The BMA is consulted on everything which is not a matter of routine administration and it negotiates with the Ministry almost every departmental decision; it is, in fact, a vital part of the departmental decision-making machinery —just as much a participant in the department in fact as the food distributors' association used to be a part of the Ministry of Food in form.[1] Only once has the Association's right to negotiate medical policy with the Ministry been questioned. That was on the occasion of the drafting of the National Health Service Act in 1945 and 1946, when Bevan 'consulted' the Association but would not consider entering into negotiations with it, at least not in the sense of giving it a virtual veto over the departmental draft. But this was a very special case, for a number of reasons. The National Health Service was an item of high policy on which a clear mandate had been given; Bevan was, in my opinion, temperamentally hostile to the medical profession; the Labour Government faced a serious problem in trying to enact its large mandate in the time available for legislation; the Future Legislation Committee of the Cabinet had devised a carefully calculated time-table for legislative projects which did not leave the Ministry much scope for dallying

[1] See R. A. Brady, *Crisis in Britain*, CUP, p. 453.

and dawdling with any BMA negotiators,[1] and the BMA's leaders had been intent upon nothing but delay since the appearance of the White Paper on a national health service. Small wonder that Bevan's refusal to 'negotiate' (but not to 'consult') proved an isolated instance. In the drafting of the National Health Service Amendment Act, for example, the profession was allowed to play a much larger role. It is true that the Minister, as a matter of constitutional principle, did not allow the BMA to see a preliminary draft of the Bill before publication (to do so would have violated Treasury rules), and it is also true that he did not put into it all the changes (but chiefly the more extravagant changes) which the BMA wanted; but the fact remains that the most important provisions of the Bill were 'negotiated' with the Association and that many of them were incorporated into it in a form the BMA had demanded.[2] Even in the case of the original National Health Service Bill only the broadest outlines of policy were removed from the area of negotiation. Bevan always conceded that anything affecting conditions of service under the scheme must be negotiated with the BMA, and, in fact, did a good deal of bargaining on his Bill, at least with certain elements of the profession. He also took a much more conciliatory attitude in regard to subordinate legislation, some of which was more important for the actual operation of the Service than the National Health Service Act itself.

On what subjects do the Ministry and Association actually consult and negotiate? What sort of business do they usually transact?

Let us begin on the lowest level of importance. Much business initiated by the BMA concerns the problems and grievances of individual practitioners. The appointment of a Registrar[3] may be threatened by a change in hospital staffing policy; through the BMA he may succeed in having his case reviewed at the level of the Ministry. A consultant may find reduced the number of sessions he is allowed under the Health Service;[4] or he may be refused a travelling allowance for trips between his home and hospital. These are the sort of things of which day-to-day business between the BMA and the Ministry chiefly consists.[5] Perhaps

---

[1] See Herbert Morrison, *Government and Parliament: A Survey from the Inside*, Oxford Univ. Press, 1954, Ch. XI.

[2] See *British Medical Journal*, 1949, I, 904 and Supp. 177.

[3] A Registrar is a qualified doctor holding a hospital position while training in a speciality: a junior specialist working on a Health Service salary.

[4] Consultants may serve whole-time or part-time under the Service. In the latter case, they are paid 'sessional fees', calculated as part-time of the whole-time salary. A 'session' is equivalent to one-eleventh of whole-time work. The maximum number of 'sessions' which may be worked part-time is nine, since part-time consultants may also engage in private practice.

[5] I have chosen individual problems which tend to occur in the specialist services as examples, in order to illustrate a point of some importance. Specialist organizations tend, significantly, to restrict their relations with the Ministry to

one should not call them unimportant, despite the lack of general public concern with such matters, for representations by the BMA are one of the chief defences medical practitioners have against injustice in administration, and that is important indeed. We tend to think too much of pressure group politics as a scrambling for special influence, as venal intrigue by the 'anonymous empire'; it may be that, but in the age of big administration and crowded legislative time-tables, interventions by voluntary organizations are also the chief control over the executive, far more thorough and efficient than question-time and adjournment debates in Parliament.

Talks on general policy are also sometimes initiated by the BMA which keeps constantly before the Ministry high documents (such as statements by the Council) on the reform of public medical policy and organization. More often than not, however, such talks are held on the initiative of the Ministry, whenever it contemplates some change in procedure. The Ministry governs the public medical services chiefly through the medium of circulars and memoranda, rather than more formal, more legally binding, statutory instruments. All such circulars and memoranda are submitted to the BMA (or joint organizations of the BMA and other bodies) before publication; many are submitted several times in the process of drafting; the vast majority are approved by the BMA (if not substantially written by it) by the time they are sent into the field.[1] This applies also to very important policy changes dignified by subordinate or amending legislation. The National Health Service Amendment Act of 1949 climaxed a long series of discussions begun already before the implementation of the National Health Service Act itself—discussions which amounted, in effect, to negotiations, despite the strong line previously taken by Bevan. As for delegated legislation, it was conceded by Bevan that the BMA or its committees should be carefully consulted on 'all points of high principle involving regulations',[2] a dogma religiously followed by subsequent Ministers of Health. Only

---

matters of high policy; routine matters and isolated grievances are left to the BMA. They are not the sort of subjects to which the august leaders of the Royal Colleges and the Joint Committee condescend. Hence, the necessity of the BMA to the specialists. Hence, also, the division between specialists and general practitioners is not usually of practical importance, for the majority of BMA—Ministry business is routine in character.

[1] To cite one example: the circular which initiated one of the negotiations described in detail below—negotiations on the curtailment of the number of Registrars employed in the hospitals—was submitted to representatives of the Joint Committee of Consultants and Specialists and to the Central Consultants and Specialists Committee long before publication; its wording was carefully discussed twice with professional representatives before its publication—apparently with professional approval. *H. C. Deb*, Dec. 15, 1950.

[2] *British Medical Journal*, 1945, II, Supp. 100.

rarely is any policy made without thorough preparatory talks between the Ministry and Association. When this is the case it usually turns out that the Ministry has consulted another professional body, such as the Central Health Services Council (established by the National Health Service Act to advise the Minister on medical subjects). But statutory advisory machinery like the Central Health Services Council is rarely used as a means for by-passing the BMA itself; consultations after all are not held merely to elicit technical knowledge but also to satisfy the corporate 'rights' of the BMA to participate in decision-making; in any case, the Association has the power to make trouble even where professional views outside of it have been thoroughly solicited.[1]

The reports of Annual Representative Meetings and of important committees like the General Medical Services Committee provide a good index to the staggeringly wide range of subjects discussed between the Ministry and Association. They paint a picture of incessant meetings on practically every conceivable aspect of medical policy and administration. To supplement generalization with concrete detail, here are two detailed lists of subjects discussed.

a. The first summarizes the more important topics (but only the more important) discussed by Ministry officials and members of the General Medical Services Committee in 1948–49;[2] they include:

remuneration of Health Service doctors (by far the most important and most time-consuming subject);

mileage allowances for rural practitioners (that is, payments for travelling long distances to administer treatment);

arrangements for the treatment of temporary residents under the Health Service;

the problem of basic salary payments[3];

the control of general practitioners' lists (to prevent multiple registrations by patients, etc.);

[1] Examples of the BMA's ability to make trouble despite professional consultations by the Ministry are hard to find, since the BMA is usually brought into the policy-making process, but one is furnished by the ban on the manufacture of heroin discussed on page 77. This decision was taken after approval by the Central Health Services Council, without consultation of either the BMA or Royal Colleges. The result was a considerable parliamentary fiasco.
[2] *British Medical Journal*, 1949, II, Supp. 100–111.
[3] See page 129.

F

administrative processes for removing names from doctors' lists (in case of multiple registry, transfer or death of patient, etc.);

fees to be paid for vaccination and immunization, services which general practitioners are not obliged to provide to Health Service patients;

forms to be used for hospital out-patients;

problems regarding certificates for juveniles and certificates enabling patients to obtain surgical corsets;

fees to be paid to doctors who dispense their own medicines to Health Service patients (e.g. many rural practitioners);

ways to order emergency appliances and drugs;

composition of the list of specially expensive appliances (which cannot be prescribed by doctors and dispensed by 'chemists' in the normal way under the Health Service but are obtainable only through the hospital and specialist part of the Service);

the supply of pessaries and Dutch caps;

the layout of Health Service prescription books;

bulk prescribing for schools and institutions;

fees to be paid general practitioners for the administration of anaesthetics;

the range of services general practitioners are normally expected to supply to expectant mothers and post-natal cases, and mileage payments in maternity cases;

the supply of sterile devices for domiciliary midwifery;

qualifications to be required of medical assistants (young, unestablished doctors) who provide maternity services;

procedures of Medical Service Committees;[1]

the range of Health Service practitioners' obligation to provide services;

[1] See note, p. 47.

relationships between general practitioners and hospitals.

b. The second list was provided me by one of the higher-ranking permanent officials of the BMA and gives an even more vivid impression of the scope of negotiations and consultations between the Association and the Ministry; it summarizes the subjects touched on *in a single week* in discussions in which my informant participated. They included:

the question of monthly payments to general practitioners in the National Health Service (Health Service doctors are paid quarterly in arrears, a fact causing considerable hardship to some of them);

procedures to be used in appeals to succeed to a vacant practice (that is, when an applicant feels his application to succeed to an established practice has been turned down unfairly by the Medical Practice Committee and appeals his case to the Ministry of Health under the Act of 1946);

questions regarding 'ophthalmic certificates' (patients who wish to have their eyes tested under the Health Service are required to obtain a certificate from a general practitioner or ophthalmic medical practitioner referring them to an optician in order to rule out 'medical' causes of their difficulties);

the supply of anti-tetanus serums to general practitioners;

questions regarding receipt forms which patients must fill out for medicines received from rural practitioners;

who is to pay for the transport of oxygen cylinders from 'chemist' to patient in case of an emergency;

questions regarding the list of appliances general practitioners may prescribe under the Service and bulk prescriptions for institutions (two recurrent subjects);

procedures to be followed in cases of alleged excessive prescribing (the Ministry operates a very complicated scheme to detect irresponsible and needlessly expensive prescribing on Health Service forms; doctors found guilty of such prescribing may be proceeded against under the disciplinary procedures of the Service, but only after a very complicated series of procedures has been gone through);

whether certain substances may be considered drugs or not (so that they may be prescribed for the usual nominal payment to Health Service patients);

the problem of finding accommodations for young doctors, caused by the housing shortage;

payment of car allowances to trainee general practitioners (those serving apprenticeships with certain specially selected general practitioners of high professional repute who are paid specially by the Ministry for their teaching);

grievances regarding the inaccessibility of hospital X-Ray facilities to local general practitioners.

It should be borne in mind that both of these lists include only the sort of subjects taken up in formal, or near-formal, meetings and by rather high-level participants. They give us no idea of the still greater range of subjects taken up quite informally, in day-to-day contact, by correspondence, telephone and friendly meeting. Even so, these lists should make clear that in the administration and formulation of medical policy the Ministry and Association form a non-statutory partnership. Socialized medicine has 'corporatized' medical practice not just in the sense of putting it under the broad direction of a government department but also in the sense of giving the corporate bodies of the medical profession much greater control over the shape and processes of medical practice.

Structure. Who participates in discussions between the Ministry and Association and what machinery for consultation and negotiation has been evolved? On the side of the Government, the participants range from Principals in the Ministry of Health (who may act quite independently in certain cases) to the Minister himself—on one or two occasions even the Prime Minister. On the side of the Association the picture is more complicated. Formally, consultations are carried out by committees. The Central Consultants and Specialists Committee (through the Joint Committee), the General Medical Services Committee, the Public Health Committee and the Compensation and Superannuation Committee deal with business under the National Health Service;[1] the Private Practice Committee, Armed Forces

[1] The Compensation and Superannuation Committee deals with questions regarding pensions paid to Health Service practitioners and compensation for goodwill in medical practices lost when the National Health Service Act of 1946 outlawed the sale of practices.

Committee, and Occupational Health Committee deal with most business arising outside of the Service. In addition, deputations of the BMA Council may also formally enter negotiations, and from time to time special negotiating committees have been created to deal with particularly important issues. All of these bodies, however, tend to be too large for the efficient transaction of business; the GMSC, for example, has nearly 60 members. In practice, most negotiations are carried out by small groups representing the committees, almost invariably composed of the *élite* of the Association: the Chairman of the Council, the more powerful Council members, and a few powerful members of committees, usually accompanied by members of the Secretariat, who may also, in minor matters, act for all practical purposes on their own. The representatives of the Association often function as the opposite numbers—one is tempted to say *alter egos*—of officials in the Ministry; the Chairman of the Council is the counterpart (roughly speaking) of the Minister of Health; the Secretary and Deputy Secretary are the opposite numbers of the Permanent Secretary and Under-Secretary, the more important members of the GMSC (and the Medical Secretary who does its staff work) of the Assistant Secretaries and Principals in charge of general medical services.[1]

We can simplify these complicated relations by distinguishing them according to levels of formality and the importance of the subjects discussed.

Despite the importance of personal contacts, a great many formal meetings take place between BMA committees and Ministry officials; these are usually attended by so many people (committee members, officials, clerks, and messengers) that they verge upon public meetings. They include both regular meetings between officials and standing committees and extraordinary sessions with special BMA Negotiating Committees. When the National Health Service Act was being drafted, for example, a very large Negotiating Committee was constituted by the BMA and other bodies to meet with Ministry officials whenever the latter would call it in.[2] The General Medical Services Committee and

---

[1] The Chairman of the Council rarely deals directly with the Minister; but this is because most negotiations proceed on the official level. When the Minister is involved in negotiations, his counterpart, generally speaking, is the Chairman.

[2] The National Health Service Negotiating Committee consisted of 16 representatives of the BMA, 3 from the Royal College of Physicians, 3 from the Royal College of Surgeons, 2 from the Royal College of Obstetricians and Gynaecologists, 3 from the Royal Scottish Medical Corporation, 2 from the Society of Medical Officers of Health, 1 from the Medical Women's Federation, and 1 from the Society of Apothecaries—a 16 to 15 majority for the BMA. References to the Committee in the *British Medical Journal* make it clear that the BMA considered it its own in a still more substantial sense than that, although the composition of the committee also illustrates the relative multiplicity of British medical organizations.

the Joint Committee for Specialists and Consultants have full dress meetings with Ministry officials about once every three months. On these occasions, however, the full complement of members does not attend. In the case of the General Medical Services Committee, the attendance usually consists of the chairman, a member of the BMA Secretariat, a clerk and three or four members of the committee (those specially concerned, or specially powerful, or, on occasion, selected at random so as to give as many members as possible a chance to 'be on the team'); on the side of the Ministry such meetings are usually attended by an Assistant Secretary and a large number of technical advisors. Among the formal consulting bodies we should perhaps also include the Central Health Services Council and its sub-committees, on which the BMA is represented along with other medical associations,[1] and certain of the National Health Service Whitley Councils. There are altogether ten Whitley Councils operating under the Service, including a General Medical Council which is sub-divided into three committees for general practitioners, consultants and specialists, and public health officers respectively. In practice, however, the Joint Committee represents the staff side on the consultants' council and the General Medical Services Committee negotiates for general practitioners, so that Whitley machinery is practically identical with normal negotiating machinery.[2]

Degrees of formality can be discerned, therefore, even in the formal machinery of negotiation, depending on whether negotiating bodies have a statutory basis, whether meetings occur regularly, and whether the full membership or only certain delegates participate. In addition there are hosts of entirely informal contacts by telephone, correspondence, over lunch, and so on; in their very nature these cannot be schematized. Now, it is an axiom of British government that the more formal a proceeding is the less important will be the business transacted; perhaps this is a general rule applying to any decision-making system, for formal procedures (recurrent meetings of large bodies operating under fixed agenda and with inflexible rules of procedure) inhibit bargaining and the free exchange of views. On the whole, the rule holds for the relationships between the BMA and the Ministry. The periodical meetings of Ministry officials and representatives of the General Medical

[1] See note, p. 47.

[2] Indeed, to be technically quite accurate, the Whitley machinery for general practitioners seems to exist only on paper. This is due to the opposition of the GMSC to negotiations under Whitley arrangements rather than through more direct, less formal and less constricting bargaining with the Ministry—perhaps also to the possibility that room might be found on a Whitley Council for larger representations of bodies other than the BMA, men over whom the BMA's leaders have less control. The other two committees seem to be functioning— still another example of the divisions between general practitioners on one hand and specialists and MOH's on the other.

Services Committee and Joint Committee are almost wholly devoted to routine matters and to the definition of problems leading to negotiations (but only leading to them); on the other hand, special meetings called by either side are usually devoted to some important matter.[1]

To be more schematic, we can classify contacts between Ministry and Association on the following levels:

a. Routine matters of policy are handled on one side by representatives of the relevant BMA committees and an Assistant Secretary and, on the other, by departmental Principals or Assistant Secretaries. Sometimes only the committee chairman and Assistant Secretary of the BMA meet the departmental officials. Formal, periodical meetings merely *discuss* such matters; *ad hoc* meetings *decide* them.

b. Routine matters of administration, such as the grievances of individual practitioners, are dealt with informally by a member of the BMA's Secretariat and the Principal concerned. These matters rarely go to a BMA committee.

c. The majority of non-routine issues, i.e. those important to the profession and the Ministry, but raising no significant political or interdepartmental questions, are dealt with, on the BMA's side, by groups usually consisting of the committee chairman concerned, an Assistant Secretary and/or the Deputy Secretary and two or three committee members (usually members of the Council); on the Ministry's side they are handled by officials up to the level of the Under-Secretary.

d. Very important matters (that is, issues which raise interdepartmental questions, especially basic questions regarding remuneration, and anything in which there might be broad public interest) are discussed with the Permanent Secretary, and sometimes the Minister, by the Chairman of the Council and the Secretary of the BMA, sometimes joined by important Council members or the Presidents of the Royal Colleges. Occasionally a full team of BMA bigwigs goes down to the Ministry; for negotiations regarding remuneration, for example, the BMA 'team' is generally composed of the Chairman of the Council, six or so Council members and the BMA's Secretary and his deputy; for talks on the call-up of doctors during the Suez situation a team of six went to the Ministry. Sometimes, however, one or two individuals, the Council chairman or the Secretary, handle such important matters, even where formal negotiation committees have been created.

[1] For an example, see *British Medical Journal*, 1948, II, Supp. 170.

e. Private conversations with the Minister take place only rarely. They are restricted to matters of political importance, of which there are very few in the area of medical policy. When they do take place, the Chairman of the Council (occasionally the Secretary of the GMSC) speaks for the BMA, sometimes on his own initiative, although he usually tries to obtain a formal delegation of full authority from the Council.

f. Even the most important negotiations are not taken outside of the department. I know of only one exception, an occasion when there was recourse to the Prime Minister himself. Early in 1957, the Government announced in Parliament that they had decided to appoint a Royal Commission to investigate the remuneration of doctors and dentists in the National Health Service. The profession's spokesmen believed this was a manoeuvre to sidetrack claims for pay increases lodged in the previous year. The chairman of the GMSC and the Joint Consultants Committee then managed to secure an interview with Harold Macmillan. They were unsuccessful in their protests against the Royal Commission, but a short time afterwards the Government announced (as balm?) interim increases in remuneration.

It will be noted that both the formality of the proceedings and the number of negotiators tends to decline as the importance of the subject discussed and the level of the participants rises. In this case, as in others, the most important pressure group activities are not carried on by formally constituted committees but by spontaneous contact among small numbers of individuals who are in a position to commit those whom they represent.

The 'Spirit' of BMA—Ministry Relations. The proper adjective for the spirit which animates the relations sketched above is 'intimate'. BMA–Ministry relations are, on the whole, strikingly close and friendly—much closer and more friendly than the publicity they have received suggests. As usual, the public is made aware of discussions between the Ministry and the BMA only when they have reached some serious impasse; and even then the Ministry usually has to take public responsibility for positions forced upon it by interdepartmental decisions which, behind the façade of the administrative system, it may oppose as fiercely as the BMA. Most negotiations, however, never become matters of public knowledge at all. They are 'intimate' not only in that they are friendly but also in that they are highly private—out of the public limelight and insulated against both interdepartmental relations and pressure from the grass roots of the profession. Officials on both sides sometimes become exasperated with one another, and their relations, sometimes for months on end, become icy and stiff; the air thickens with charges and counter-charges; each side is said to misunderstand the other, to be obstinate and unreasonable. But one must classify such tiffs as aberrations. They are the sort of quarrels inevitable among the best of friends and partners. Moreover, the area of tension is always very small. It is confined to one or two special areas in which the relations between the officials of the Ministry and the BMA are not 'closed' but subject to external pressures —on one side from powerful governmental departments, on the other from the rank and file of the profession—so that both sets of officials become mere deputies for invisible antagonists and lose their normal freedom of accommodation. As we shall see, this is particularly the case in that touchiest of all areas of policy: remuneration.

Except for the very brief periods of sulking and irritation on both sides, officials of the Ministry and the BMA certainly do not behave like persistent antagonists. Much telephoning, lunching, and corresponding takes place among them. In unguarded moments, officials of the BMA sometimes refer to Ministry officials as 'our colleagues', and most of them seem to be on first-name terms—something which is rather more significant in Britain than in the United States. There is even, according to one of my informants, an annual joint cocktail party, given just before Christmas at BMA House in Tavistock Square; but I do not know whether this piece of information is apocryphal or not. Still more to the point is the fact that among the two sets of officials there operates what the British call a 'backstairs network'. While publicity of some negotiations does find its way into Parliament, and the public media, any genuinely difficult negotiations are, as far as one can gather, talked out as much as possible 'on the backstairs', at least until there is a genuine breakdown of negotiations. Then, of course, public statements are made, negotiating committees swing into action, and the Minister is dragged into the discussions; but this happens impressively rarely. On the whole, officials on both sides are probably on better terms personally than in their official capacities, but that seems chiefly due to factors which compel them in certain negotiations to assume belligerent poses. It also appears true that the higher up one goes in both hierarchies the less cordial are the personal feelings of the men involved toward one another; that, however, is also natural, since the great leaders come into play chiefly in the more difficult and exasperating negotiations and consultations.

It is important to realize that the spirit of BMA–Ministry relations has tended to remain constant under different Ministers, whether hostile (like Aneurin Bevan) or friendly (like most of the rest). We may suspect therefore that this spirit is something arising 'naturally' out of the situation in which BMA–Ministry relations take place. What are the relevant elements of this situation? First, perhaps, is the very fact that Ministers do not very often intrude upon the affairs of the Ministry and Association, a fact due in turn to the low political volatility of medical policy at present; like interdepartmental pressures, political considerations would not only make for inconsistency in BMA–Ministry relations but would also serve to tie the hands of the Ministry's officials and exasperate those with whom they deal. Even more important, both sides are constantly thrown together and, what is more, indispensable to one another. A real breakdown of the relationships would be intolerable to one as much as to the other. The Ministry controls the conditions of medical practice; how then could the profession's chief corporate instrument risk antagonizing it beyond safe limits? The Ministry, moreover, is necessary to the BMA as its advocate before other government departments and at the level of the Cabinet, particularly on questions of expenditure. And the very pretensions of the Association to represent the profession monolithically depends upon the maintenance of close relations with the Ministry. On the other hand the Association is equally useful to the Ministry: as a source of technical information, as a channel through which to educate and reconcile practitioners, and, not least, because the support of the Association is one of the few power factors the Ministry can exert in interdepartmental disputes or under political fire. Finally, we must emphasize once again the broad consensus on medical policy which provides common ground in disputes and minimizes external pressures.

All this is underlined by an instructive paradox: on the whole, relations between the Ministry and the Association seem to me to have been even smoother under a hostile Minister (Bevan) than they have been under his more cordial successors.[1] Some reasons for this have already been mentioned, but others may be added. Bevan had to bring the National Health Service into existence, and while, during the stage of drafting legislation, that required a high-handed attitude, it required close collaboration in the stage of implementation—close collaboration in the interest of both sides. Nor must we forget that both sides—despite the highly publicized disputes which ushered in the National Health Service—were then committed to an important job of medical reform on which they and the whole country were agreed,[2] while today attention is focused on the less inspiring, more exasperating, details of administrative repairs and adjustments.

We have often been told that relationships between British civil servants and pressure group officials are intimate primarily for social reasons: that there is in Great Britain an 'old boy network' of men who

[1] See above, Ch. II, pp. 55-56.
[2] See Eckstein, *The English Health Service*, Ch. 5 and 6.

have all been to certain Public Schools, who have similar tastes and accents, who belong to the same clubs, occupy similar preferred positions on the social stratification scale, move in the same social circles, and are for all these reasons close intimates. Undoubtedly this network exists, and, more often than not, it moves the wheels of government. But, the range of backgrounds and associations one encounters when dealing with BMA and Ministry of Health officials strongly suggests that there is much more to the backstairs network than social structure. The network exists for many reasons. The pattern of policy makes necessary continuous and constructive relations between government officials and those of voluntary associations. British 'political culture',[1] especially consensus, acts as a powerful cement in all British political relations. Not least, the British structure of authority in government and voluntary associations, permits continuous relationships, in a 'closed' setting, between clearly defined and highly delimited sets of decision-makers, wielding power sufficient for smooth accommodation and effective compromise.

[1] S. H. Beer, in *Patterns of Government: The Major Political Systems of Europe*, pp. 12–25, defines this term.

IV

The Political Effectiveness of the BMA

The political power of the BMA is determined, as always, by a ratio between positive and negative factors: factors extending and factors limiting its influence. On the positive side are, above all, its pre-eminent position in the corporate structure of the medical profession and its intimate relations with the Ministry; alongside these must be cited its command of indispensable technical knowledge and professional prestige, certain aspects of its internal power structure, and the non-controversial character of most public medical policies. On the negative side belong certain divisions within the Association, its lack of absolute size (hence inability to mobilize electoral considerations), the inferior position of the Ministry of Health in the interdepartmental power-structure, and normative inhibitions in the medical profession against certain types of political pressure and against 'trade union' methods. But from this we can deduce little more than that the BMA is an effective pressure group and that its influence must have important limits. It remains to determine more precisely the boundaries of its political effectiveness and to weight the influence of the various power factors in particular negotiations. This is done best by beginning with a review of some concrete political failures and successes of the Association.

Some Notable Failures

A superficial reading of the history of the BMA in politics might seem to confirm one of the hoary and misleading clichés of political science: that British interest groups are relatively ineffective, and therefore unimportant, because of the concentration of decision-making powers in the Cabinet, a body more insulated than other important democratic decision-making bodies against interest group pressure. The plain fact is that the BMA has lost all the crucial public disputes over medical policy in which it has engaged during this century. Twice the government has passed over BMA opposition legislation affecting the whole structure of medicine—opposition which was intense despite the broad area of agreement between the profession and the Government. From this standpoint the BMA emerges as a pressure group considerably weaker than the American Medical Association, which has managed to stop (among others) a national health insurance bill championed by a popular President in the very flush of electoral victory.

Consider briefly the pre-natal history of the National Health Service Act of 1946 as an exercise in the limitations of the BMA's powers. That the BMA did not oppose root and branch the scheme for socialized medicine proposed in the White Paper of 1944 we already know. It did, however, oppose many aspects of it, particularly certain projected administrative arrangements (rather than broad principles). Also, opposition to the Government's scheme was much more intense among the BMA's leaders and officials than among the rank and file, and the leaders had no trouble making their more recalcitrant position official policy.[1] The speed with which the Labour government made for the statute books after the election of 1945 goaded them into a desperate resistance, but the effect was not even sufficient to slow the Labour government down. Not only did the Bill go through Parliament as planned, but in devising it, as I have already pointed out, the Minister and his officials paid little heed to the BMA's (for once well-publicized) views. A large National Health Service Negotiating Committee was created, chiefly under BMA auspices, to do what its title suggests, but Bevan was not available for negotiations. He did hold some twenty conferences on the bill with various interested parties, including the medical profession, (in addition to representatives of the dental profession, pharmacists, nurses, midwives, opticians, medical aid societies and herbalists) and his officials held thirteen more,[2] but an important Labour spokesman (Herbert Morrison) pointed out in one of the debates on the Bill that the Minister did not consider these conferences to be

[1] This is a good example of the distribution of power within the BMA. There can be no question that the BMA leaders' feelings toward a socialized medical service cooled considerably after the appearance of the Beveridge Report in 1942, although they had been in the forefront of the agitation for medical reform up to that time. When the White Paper outlining the coalition government's plan for a national health service appeared in 1944, the BMA's leaders, confident that their negative views were shared by the rank and file, distributed a 'Questionary' to the profession eliciting its views on the proposals, in general and detail. The results came as something of a shock. Despite the fact that a majority were opposed to the scheme as a whole, there were large majorities in favour of many of the more controversial proposals. The leaders now disavowed the reliability of the poll they had sponsored and gave responsibility for the definition of the Association's policy to the Annual Representative Meeting, which in fact took a less accommodating line. Subsequently, the lead was taken by the Council and, after that, by an even more exclusive body, the Negotiating Committee on the National Health Service. (See note 2, p. 85.) The power to speak for the profession was thus gradually transferred from the membership as such to a body in which older, established general practitioners were more heavily represented than other groups within the profession, and from these to the normal political *élite* of the profession. For a more detailed discussion see Eckstein, *The English Health Service*, pp. 143–157.

[2] *H. C. Deb*, April 30, 1946.

'negotiations'.[1] This is confirmed by the reports of the discussions which have leaked out. The conferences appear to have been anything but bargaining sessions. The Minister is alleged to have received the Negotiating Committee 'with the silent disdain of a nineteenth century capitalist meeting a deputation of his employees'[2] and a spirit of *ipse dixitism* apparently ruled his consultations. The profession's 'negotiators'—who were allowed to cool their heels for a considerable time as Bevan went to meetings at BMA House and those of other professional bodies to deliver charming, self-effacing speeches, while his officials secretly began drafting the Bill—were called in from time to time and confronted by virtual *faits accomplis*. The Minister was perfectly willing to haggle over 'details' (that is, regulations to be made after enactment of the Bill), but not over the outlines of his scheme.[3] Enjoining the utmost secrecy upon the Negotiating Committee he revealed the more important proposals as they matured. The members of the Committee made comments and criticisms; the Minister listened but 'withheld his response';[4] he never argued. Furthermore, he treated the negotiators not as representatives of the medical corporations but as specially qualified individuals whose views it seemed worthwhile to elicit:[5] this clearly in order to check at the outset any belief that the medical corporations had the right to participate in the legislative process. As a result, only a week before the Bill was introduced in the House of Commons the BMA still seemed to be in the dark about the provisions it would ultimately contain.[6] In the end these provisions were not so very different from what the BMA had wanted; but for the time being the good relations which generally result from being on common ground were not established, due to the impact of procedural differences; in the case of the Minister himself, in fact, good personal relations were never to be re-established.

All this was nothing new, but a repetition of the unfortunate history of the National Health Insurance Act of 1911. Lloyd George then treated the BMA with even more haughty disregard than Aneurin Bevan. He did not even 'consult' it in drafting his proposals and he included in these proposals many arrangements to which the profession had long been opposed.[7] The result was serious talk about a professional boycott of the Service, but even this was ineffectual in budging Lloyd George. He did make concessions on points of detail, but not on the

---

[1] *H. C. Deb.*, April 8, 1946.
[2] *British Medical Journal*, 1946, I, Supp. 55.
[3] *Lancet*, 1946, II, 719.
[4] *British Medical Journal*, 1946, I, 240.
[5] *H. C. Deb.*, April 8, 1946.
[6] *British Medical Journal*, 1946, I, 59.
[7] See Eckstein, *The English Health Service.* p. 127.

scheme as such. In 1946 opposition did not go quite so far; still, it went pretty far. A defence fund was created to propagandize the profession and public and to help out individual recalcitrant doctors.[1] Plebiscites were arranged (on rather loaded questions) to voice the profession's corporate disapproval. The effect, in the end, was much the same as in 1911: victories on details, indeed striking victories, but only on details; the implementation of the National Health Service Act was not even delayed.[2]

Since then the BMA has had to take its lumps in important negotiations too. The most notorious of all negotiations after 1948 have been about remuneration. In these the BMA has never been treated so summarily as it was on the National Health Insurance and National Health Service Bills; still, the Ministry has made unusual difficulties in negotiations about pay and the BMA has never managed to get more than a part of what it wanted, either in money or in machinery for settling disputes about remuneration.[3] Feelings have been strained at times to fever pitch by the obstacles to settlement thrown up by the Ministry; strikes (i.e. mass withdrawals from the National Health Service) have been threatened; discussions have been broken off and arbitration called for, signalling the breakdown of good relations. Under these pressures the Ministry has occasionally made concessions, such as calling upon outside parties to suggest means of settling a dispute; but these concessions have certainly not been tantamount to capitulation and remuneration has remained the chief area of tension between the Ministry and the Association.[4]

In addition to remuneration, there are three other areas in which the Ministry of Health has proved relatively stubborn and unyielding. It has been obstinate, first, about any demands requiring new legislation. The BMA has pried one National Health Service Amendment Act out of it, but usually discussions on points requiring parliamentary action have been put off or explicitly turned down. A case in point is the obstinacy of the Ministry in regard to introducing something like the University Grants system to finance Health Service hospitals. It was widely felt in the profession that annual hospital budgets were too constricting to permit efficient hospital administration and that grants for several years, like those given the universities, were more desirable; but, despite pressures from the BMA, the Royal Colleges and the

---

[1] *Lancet*, 1946, I, 354.

[2] A discussion of the profession's reaction to the Act of 1946 is given in Ross, *National Health Service in Great Britain*, pp. 122–27.

[3] For example, the Ministry has never agreed to the BMA's proposal that all negotiations about remuneration should automatically go to an arbitration tribunal.

[4] For a detailed study of a series of negotiations about remuneration, see Chapter VI below.

Institute of Hospital Administrators, the Ministry has never yielded one inch on this subject. The Ministry has also proved unyielding on proposals that would promote private practice alongside the National Health Service. Here the record of the BMA's achievements is not quite so bleak[1] but many important requests have been turned down: for example, the BMA's proposal that doctors should be allowed themselves to determine the scale of fees paid by patients using pay-beds in Health Service hospitals.[2] Finally, the BMA has had greater difficulty in negotiations concerning specialists than general practitioners, although here the difficulty is not so much due to the Ministry's obstinacy as to the inability of the BMA to get its way in cases of disagreement with the Royal Colleges and Joint Committee.

Achievements

Almost all the areas of policy in which the BMA has been relatively ineffective are basic and important areas: the statutes organizing the medical services, changes calling for further legislation, the balance between public and private practice, and the most important trade-union activity of the Association, pressure for greater remuneration. One may be led to conclude that on the big issues the BMA has proved extraordinarily impotent. But this would be a hasty and ill-advised conclusion, one requiring such drastic modifications as to be hardly serviceable at all. Behind the record of public failures is a much more impressive record of not-so-public successes, greatest of all on minor matters, points of 'detail', but impressive enough also in the case of 'principles'. To get a more balanced view of the BMA's political effectiveness, let us look at its achievements in regard to the National Health Service Act, from its introduction into Parliament in March of 1946 to its coming into operation in July of 1948.

While the Minister of Health adamantly refused to concede to the medical profession a right to participate in drafting legislation, he did begin making important concessions to it even before the introduction of the National Health Service Bill in Parliament. For example, we have reason to think that the initial plans of the Ministry called for a fully integrated hospital service, a service in which all hospitals would be grouped in large regions and their operations planned and integrated by specially created Regional Hospital Boards. In the end, however, the

---

[1] For some concessions to private practice, see below, pp. 105.

[2] Some accommodation for the private patients of Health Service specialists has been set aside in Health Service hospitals. Patients pay the full cost of maintaining the beds concerned and their doctor's fees. However, maximum fees are laid down in Regulations to prevent any undue exploitation of these facilities. See the *National Health Service (Pay-Bed Accommodation in Hospitals, etc.) Regulations*, S. I, 1948, No. 1490.

most important of all the hospitals—teaching hospitals—were placed outside the jurisdiction of the Regional Hospital Boards and given independent administrative authorities of their own, the Boards of Governors, thus corrupting at the outset the principle of overall regional planning. There can be little doubt that this change was made to appease certain important medical groups, especially the higher ranks of consultants working in the teaching hospitals who wanted to prevent any debasement of their hospitals' status *vis-à-vis* others through integrated hospital planning. Before the bill was introduced a medical demand that private practice should be allowed in National Health Service hospitals (in the so-called pay-beds) seems also to have been granted.[1] Perhaps we should not make too much of these pre-parliamentary concessions; in an oblique way they illustrate the weakness of the BMA better perhaps than its strength, for all of them were clearly made to urge the specialists into a favourable position and thereby to weaken the medical profession's front at its most vulnerable point. Still, even if granted for tactical reasons, these concessions were welcome to most of the profession, and it is certainly an asset to be able to compel even tactical concessions. At any rate, the pre-parliamentary concessions were portents of a much more obliging attitude on the part of the Minister once the hard job of getting legislation before Parliament had been done.

Many concessions to broader medical opinion were made during the parliamentary debates. They are far too numerous to list completely, but let us take a look at some of them. One important series of concessions was made during the committee stage in the House of Commons, the stage at which draft legislation is usually most broadly revised. Certain changes were made in the position of the Minister's professional advisory body, the Central Health Services Council; the power of Hospital Management Committees to receive and use at discretion voluntary gifts was guaranteed;[2] the right of admitting patients and providing treatment in private wards was extended from specialists to *all* Health Service practitioners; and a clause was inserted to guarantee that anyone serving on a National Health Service Committee would not be deprived of any civil rights, such as the right to stand for Parliament.[3] A further series of such concessions was made at the eleventh hour, during the debate on third reading in the House of Lords: the Minister

[1] The relevant provisions are *National Health Service Act* 1946, Sec. 11 and Third Schedule and (for pay-beds), Sec. 5 and *National Health Service (Pay-Bed Accommodation in Hospitals) Regulations*, S. I, 1948, No. 1490.

[2] The Regional Hospital Boards previously mentioned are, broadly speaking, planning bodies; under their jurisdiction Hospital Management Committees actually perform the day-to-day administration of the hospitals. *National Health Service Act*, 1946, Sec. 11 and *National Health Service (Functions of Regional Hospital Boards, etc.) Regulations*, S. I, 1948, No. 60.

[3] For further details of these concessions, see the *Lancet*, 1946, II, 163.

G

conceded that the objects of hospital endowments taken over by the Ministry should be respected as far as possible,[1] that the religious associations of denominational hospitals incorporated into the Service should be preserved, and that a practitioner called before the Health Service Tribunal[2] should be permitted to have legal counsel, to call witnesses and to have his hearing in public upon request. During other parliamentary stages the Minister, or other government spokesmen, agreed not to alter the composition of the Central Health Services Council[3] by mere executive fiat but to bring all such changes before the House, and that the Medical Practices Committee,[4] in considering applicants for vacant practices, was to give special regard to the desires of the previous incumbent practitioners and first preference to any relatives. Not all of these concessions were written into the Act, but all that were left out found their way into Regulations or into the Amendment Act of 1949.

Perhaps the largest concession made during the parliamentary stages of the National Health Service Bill (or very shortly after)[5] concerned the remuneration of general practitioners. This also happened to be the chief source of disquiet with the Bill in BMA House. The leadership of the Association was worried, first of all, over the possibility of a whole-time salaried medical service: a service in which family doctors would be compelled to devote their full time to public medical practice in return for the payment of a fixed salary. Opposition to such a system of remuneration was Principle I of the set of basic principles drawn up by the Health Service Negotiating Committee.[6] Bevan insisted that he had no intention of introducing such a service under the wide discretion given the Minister in the Bill to settle terms of service for general medical practitioners, but the BMA leadership was not satisfied with assurances. It wanted, and got, an Amendment Act which, among other concessions, prohibited legally any full-time salaried service of general medical or general dental practitioners.[7] Much of this Act, it should be noted, was

[1] All endowments held by voluntary hospitals on the 'appointed day' of the Health Service were vested in the Minister free of any trust. A Hospital Endowment Fund was established to administer the funds so acquired, in order to distribute them more evenly among the hospitals, but the Minister agreed, under prodding, to take into consideration the original wishes of the donors in distributing proceeds from the Fund. *National Health Service Act*, 1946, Sec. 7.

[2] See note, p. 48.

[3] See note, p. 47.

[4] See note, p. 46.

[5] Some concessions were promised during the parliamentary course of the Bill but, for the sake of expedition, left to be dealt with formally after the Bill had passed.

[6] *British Medical Journal*, 1946, I, 468.

[7] *National Health Service (Amendment) Act*, 1949, 12, 13 & 14, Geo. 6 c. 93, Sec. 10. The other concessions also suggest appeasement of the general practitioner part of the Service. Apart from clarifying certain very obscure provisions

negotiated with the profession, on the Minister's own admission, suggesting that the refusal to negotiate the original Act was not so much a matter of principle as of expediency (speed).[1]

The second major source of anxiety about remuneration centred on the issue of a 'basic salary' for general medical practitioners. Although the Minister had promised not to introduce a whole-time salaried service he clearly seemed to want a system of remuneration under which general practitioners would be paid chiefly by salary, plus small capitation fees; at least so he said during the committee stage of the Health Service Bill.[2] Under pressure, however, he gradually gave way before the BMA. We can follow the retreat almost step by step. First, Bevan explains that he merely wants the basic salary to be 'a large part', not necessarily the major part, of every general practitioner's income; some weeks later he says that it should be paid only to doctors whose capitation fees would not bring them up to a certain minimum income; then, he proposes that payment of a basic salary should be limited to three years, after which it would be up to each doctor to decide whether to continue it or not; shortly after that, regulations are published which circumscribe the basic salary even more, indeed, limit it nearly out of existence: payment of a basic salary is now to be made only to doctors who elect to receive it in the first place and who obtain the approval of the Executive Council after consultations with the local Medical Committee (approval which, under the overall method of remuneration adopted, was likely to be granted only in unusual cases).[3] Finally, following up the Regulations, the Ministry issues a circular explicitly instructing the Executive Councils to grant basic salaries only in certain cases: when a general practi-

---

regarding partnerships and the employment of assistants which had created a a great deal of concern among general practitioners, the Amendment Act created special panels of practitioners to sit on the Tribunal, so that practitioners would not be tried by people entirely unqualified in their field, and gave the Executive Councils the right to choose their own chairmen. Most interesting of all, the Act gave the Executive Councils the power to deduct the expenses of Local Medical Committees from the remuneration of general practitioners, a provision badly wanted by the BMA since it meant, in effect, the compulsory collection of dues for at least some local 'BMA' activities—not in form, but certainly in effect. (See p. 47.)

[1] The Minister certainly gave the impression in Parliament that he was actively negotiating with the BMA over the provisions of the Amending Act. (See, for example, *H. C. Deb.*, Dec. 2, 1948.) The profession, on the other hand, received the Act in rather bad grace since it did not grant a few minor things it had wanted, e.g. permission to doctors' private patients to obtain drugs at public expense. (See *Brit. Med. J.*, 1949, I, 904, for the BMA's attitudes.) Others complained, however, that the Amendment Act had gone much too far towards meeting the demands of the profession. (For an example, see *H. C. Deb.*, May 24, 1949.)

[2] *H. C. Deb.*, June 18, 1946.

[3] For the reason, see pp. 129-130. The pertinent regulations are the *National Health Service (General Medical and Pharmaceutical Services) Regulations*, S. I, 1948, No. 506, Schedule I, Part II.

tioner is starting a new practice, when he is disabled by ill health, and
so on. By the end of 1948, then, the BMA had become peacefully reconciled to the idea of a basic salary; the Ministry, in fact, was no longer
talking about 'basic salaries' at all, but, in deference to BMA sensibilities
one suspects, about 'fixed annual payments'. Later still, further
concessions to the BMA were made and the fixed annual payments
transformed into 'initial practice allowances', a still less offensive term.

This relentless retreat of the Ministry on the issue of basic salaries
was typical of its behaviour during the whole two years between the
enactment of the Bill and the beginning of the operation of the National
Health Service. Where Bevan had been adamant before, he became
accommodating now. His attitude became conciliatory; he was willing,
even anxious, to negotiate the terms of the Health Service Regulations.
Nothing illustrates the great extent of the BMA's political power more
vividly than the history of the National Health Service Regulations
before the appointed day of the Service. An overall sketch of this
history may be instructive, even though I have touched already on some
aspects of it.

The cavalier treatment of the profession's representatives during the
drafting of the National Health Service Bill led to repercussions that
threatened to sabotage the Act before it could be brought into operation.
Shortly after the Health Service Act received the royal assent a plebiscite
was held asking the profession whether it desired the Negotiating
Committee to enter into discussion with the Minister regarding Regulations; implicit in this question, as the BMA itself pointed out, was the
question of whether the profession was to operate the Service at all. The
result was a 55 per cent majority against negotiations, a serious, although
not exactly devastating, result (not devastating because 20 per cent of
those polled abstained).[1] That the result was not more ominous still was
due chiefly to the radicalism of the specialists; 64 per cent of the general
practitioners voted no. Even so, a crisis of confidence existed, although
the BMA's leaders had pledged themselves to accept the result only in
the event of a 'sufficient majority'. In this crisis it was once more the
specialist part of the profession which smoothed things over. The
Presidents of the Royal Colleges wrote to the Minister asking for a
clarification of views on issues which particularly bothered the profession: remuneration, the composition and operation of the Tribunal, and
the practitioner's liberty of movement under the Service.[2] The Minister
grasped the opportunity to make a conciliatory declaration promising
important concessions on all of these issues and stating that he really

[1] See Ross, *National Health Service in Great Britain*, pp. 122–27, a good
discussion of the whole period from the passage of the Bill to the appointed day.
[2] Letter dated January 2, 1947.

wanted to have the profession's help and advice.[1] About a week later the BMA Council met and decided to enter into negotiations after all, prodded no doubt by the fact that the Minister and his officials had already gone ahead with drafting Regulations on their own,[2] and a Special Representative Meeting was convened to approve the Council's decision: shortly thereafter, the Minister explicitly agreed to 'negotiations'.[3] A new negotiating committee, a majority of which—and the chairman—were leaders of the BMA, was now organized and divided, for purposes of discussions, into six sub-committees;[4] about the same time, the BMA, in a symbolic gesture of reconciliation, complied with the Minister's request to nominate members to the newly created Regional Hospital Boards. This marked the end of the first phase of the period we are reviewing. The Minister had been prodded down from his haughty position regarding negotiations; the Association had been persuaded to co-operate in the implementation of the new Service.

Intensive discussions now went on for some eight months (until October 1947). These discussions were secret, but we can reconstruct in broad outline who carried them on and what subjects were discussed. The sub-committees of the National Health Service Negotiating Committee negotiated for the profession with senior officials of the Ministry, the lead being taken by H. Guy Dain and Charles Hill, the Chairman of Council and Secretary of the BMA respectively. On the BMA's insistence, talks concerned not only the Regulations to be made under the Act but also amending legislation, hence principles as well as details. In short, what the BMA had been denied during the drafting of the National Health Service Bill it got immediately after its enactment: a voice in determining the statutory provisions relating to the Health Service, though not an absolutely decisive vote. What was granted, in effect, was the right to argue a case rather than merely to present it, and

---

[1] *British Medical Journal*, 1947, I, 66.
[2] For example, the order determining hospital regions was issued during this period. *National Health Service (Determination of Regional Hospital Areas)* Order SR & O 1946, No. 2158. This was a matter of particular concern to specialists; hence, perhaps, the intervention of the three Presidents.
[3] *British Medical Journal*, 1947, I, 227 and Supp. 18.
[4] The exact composition was as follows:
18 representatives of the BMA.
13 representatives of the Royal College of Physicians
3 representatives of the Royal College of Surgeons
2 representatives of the Royal College of Obstetricians and Gynaecologists
3 representatives of the Royal Scottish Medical Corporations
1 representative of the Medical Women's Federation
1 representative of the Society of Apothecaries
1 representative of the Association of Honorary Staffs of the Major Voluntary Hospitals.
Some of the non-BMA representatives may also be reckoned, for practical purposes, as BMA spokesmen. (*Brit. Med. J.*, 1947, I, Supp. 27.)

an assurance that agreement with the profession would be earnestly sought, not just that its views would be taken into consideration. Even so, another crisis of confidence had to be surmounted before a full reconciliation could be achieved.

To appreciate the political successes of the BMA during this period one should be aware of the more important issues at stake in the negotiations. The basic issues concerned the provisions of the Act relating to partnership agreements (Section 35)—mostly technical matters which needed clarification more than revision; provisions regarding the buying and selling of practices (outlawed by the Health Service Act); and a problem already discussed, the question of basic salaries in the general practitioners' remuneration. These seem to have been the chief subjects of discussion, but many others were frequently touched upon: whether, for example, all or only specially qualified practitioners should be allowed to practice midwifery under the Health Service Act; whether the Minister or the Executive Councils themselves should appoint Executive Council chairmen; whether an appeal to the Courts from the Tribunal's decisions would be allowed; whether the Regional Hospital Boards should be compelled to consult local medical committees on appointments to Hospital Management Committees; whether the maximum number of patients permitted to register with an individual doctor should be 4,000 or fewer; whether all specialists should be allowed to carry on private practice in private hospitals, or only those permitted to do so by the Minister; whether local Health Committees (that is, sub-committees of ordinary local government authorities in charge of medical services still administered by these authorities) should be required, not merely permitted, to co-opt medical members; and so on—we need not recite the whole long and tedious list.[1]

The whole case of the negotiating committee was published in December of 1947. At the same time the Minister published his comments. He conceded almost everything the committee had wanted. Yes, the obscure passages on partnerships in the Act would be clarified; no, general practitioners would not be barred from providing maternity services; Executive Councils would appoint their own chairmen; practitioners would be allowed to carry up to 4,000 patients each;—right down the list of the negotiating committee's demands the Ministry gave in, promising implementation of its concessions in the Regulations.[2] What was not conceded? In the end, only three points of the profession's case: amending legislation was to be considered but it was not 'promised'; the Minister's retreat from the basic salary had not yet gone

---

[1] For a list of issues, see British Medical Journal, 1947, II, Supp. 141–51 and 777–78.
[2] British Medical Journal, 1947, II, 154–62.

quite far enough to suit the committee; and some minor demands regarding control by the Medical Practices Committee over the distribution of general practitioners had been refused. Among these issues the demand for an amending act (to guarantee by statute concessions already assured) loomed by far the largest, and over this demand a new 'crisis' was generated.

In 1911, Lloyd George, having ignored the profession while drafting legislation, conceded all its demands afterwards;[1] nevertheless opposition to his scheme ran so high that the BMA wanted to boycott it even after its victory. This is exactly what happened early in 1948. Feelings on the unresolved issues became exacerbated on both sides; on the part of the profession a new plebiscite produced a 90 per cent vote against the Service in the form it then had, while from the Ministry were heard ominous rumblings about 'sabotage' of the law.[2] But cooler heads soon prevailed: neither side was at this point willing to risk an irrevocable falling out. Some weeks after the plebiscite Guy Dain, the Chairman of the Council, made some conciliatory remarks before a special Representative Meeting of the BMA; shortly after, Aneurin Bevan reciprocated in the House of Commons. Bevan at this point made one of his well-judged retreats on the question of basic salaries; he created a committee to review certain unresolved issues on medical partnerships, including the two lawyers who had prepared the BMA's case on this matter; most important, he gave definite assurances that an amending act would be introduced granting the most important changes the BMA had wanted. The very next day, the National Health Service Committee of the BMA asked Bevan to receive a delegation and negotiations were resumed, culminating in the Amendment Act of 1949. The profession's leaders now dropped all threats of boycott and the BMA Council advised doctors to enter the Health Service—small wonder, considering that the negotiating committee had extracted important concessions on nearly every aspect of its case, some guaranteed by legislation which it helped, in fact, to write.[3]

It may be wondered why Bevan was so adamant toward the BMA while legislation was being prepared and so willing to give in to it, even to the point of implicitly modifying one or two of the Act's provisions, after the Health Service Act had been passed. One explanation is that the

[1] Eckstein, *The English Health Service*, p. 127.
[2] *British Medical Journal*, 1948, I, 353.
[3] If I have followed the negotiations correctly only one demand by the profession was completely denied in the end: that an appeal should be permitted from the Tribunal to the regular courts. But important concessions were made on the composition of the Tribunal, to guarantee legal processes and the presence of a registered practitioner on every board adjudicating a case. Under the final version of the NHS Act practitioners are entitled to legal counsel in Tribunal proceedings.

first attitude represented a functional adjustment (as the sociologists call it) to the need to get some sort of coherent legislation on the statute book, while the second represented a similar adjustment to the need to get a working service into operation. Another explanation—which bears on a point previously discussed (Bevan's power as Minister of Health)—is that he had relatively little authority over the drafting of the Bill, but much more over its implementation. Until 1947, broad co-ordinating power over the social services was vested in a committee of the Cabinet, the Social Services Committee, under the direction of Arthur Greenwood, a man of much greater influence than is now generally attributed to him.[1] In addition, Viscount Addison, a medical man, undoubtedly exerted much influence in the shaping of medical policy, particularly since he was very close to Attlee, closer perhaps than any politician other than Bevin and Cripps. Finally, it should be remembered that a Health Service was also being planned for Scotland, and that the Secretary of State for Scotland must have had an important voice in the overall shaping of policy. One may infer from this that the adamant Bevan was adamant just because his own freedom of manoeuvre in consultations was limited; that he appeared as the representative of the policy-making authorities rather than as the authoritative policy-maker in his own person. But once the shape of the Service had been decided and the Bill passed, committee government ceased to operate with the same constricting force and Bevan's freedom to make concessions became much greater; he then became Bevan the negotiator. Again, of course, these two considerations are not mutually exclusive, nor indeed unrelated to one another.

It would not be very useful to catalogue all the political achievements of the BMA since the Act came into operation. Suffice it to say that the experience of 1946–48 provides a good sample of what has followed. On important points the profession's leaders have been able consistently to get their way, save only for one conspicuous exception (remuneration), so that one can accurately say that the National Health Service Act in operation is to a large extent a joint enterprise of the BMA and the Ministry, however intransigent the Ministry was at its birth. It would be a useless exaggeration to say that the BMA always gets what it wants. If we compare the formal lists of demands it has drawn up from time to time[2] with concessions actually achieved the discrepancy may in fact seem large. But these lists are usually drawn up by the representative organs and represent little more than catalogues of popular grievances, or they are lists drawn up by the Council to show to the rank and file that it is busily on its toes; they rarely govern actual transactions with the

[1] See Herbert Morrison, *Government and Parliament*, 1954, pp. 20–21.
[2] See, e.g. *British Medical Journal*, 1952, I, Supp. 1.

Ministry. In such transactions the BMA's achievements far, far out-weigh its failures.[1]

Determinants of Achievements and Failures

How can we reconcile the striking political setbacks which the BMA has suffered on some occasions with its remarkable effectiveness on other occasions ? And how has the BMA managed to gain, in the process of day-to-day negotiations under the statutes, many of the points apparently denied it by the statutes themselves ?

We certainly cannot account for its successes and failures through accidental human factors, that is, through the different attitudes and tempers of different Ministers of Health. The record under Bevan alone is quite as inconsistent as the overall balance-sheet; on certain issues the Ministry has proved accommodating or recalcitrant under all Ministers; the structure of BMA–Ministry relations has, as we already know, remained very much the same since 1946; and Ministers do not usually make so great an impact on their departments as to upset the whole network of practices and relations previously established. One must try to explain the BMA's political successes and failures through persistent, non-accidental factors, rather than the vagaries of personal dispositions.

[1] Here is a very abbreviated list of some important concessions gained by the profession since 1948:
1. Transformation of the fixed annual payments into 'initial practice allowances' —involving not only a change in name but a further restriction in the basic salaries paid to certain practitioners.
2. Exemption of 15 per cent of all pay-beds on Health Service premises from the maximum fees which, under the Regulations, doctors may charge to patients using such beds.
3. A compulsory levy on Health Service doctors to finance the local Medical Committees.
4. The exemption of Registrar establishments from central qualitative control and an expansion in the number of Senior Registrars whose employment is permitted in Health Service hospitals. (See below, pp. 114-123, for details.)
5. Instructions to the Medical Practices Committee to count doctors' assistants in calculating the adequacy of the number of doctors in various parts of Britain— a provision which makes it more difficult for young doctors to establish new practices, both by closing areas previously open and restricting the payment of initial practice allowances.
6. A provision to allow private practice in Health Centres under the National Health Service.
7. Increases in the mileage fund for rural practitioners.
8. Payment of travelling allowances to Registrars.
9. Permission to specialists practising whole-time under the Health Service to provide domiciliary consultations at extra charge.
These gains are reflected in the tone of reports from the committees representing the profession at the Ministry, which have become increasingly self-congratula-tory since 1948. Already in 1949 the Chairman of the General Medical Services Committee was able to report placidly to the Conference of Representatives of Local Medical Committees: 'The Committee has had a strenuous year. . . . As GPs they had lost no ground with the Ministry and they had made some gains' —a vast understatement. (*Brit. Med. J.*, 1949, II, Supp. 199.)

Failures. The general principle illustrated most clearly by the failures of the BMA is the obvious one that British pressure groups, due to the structure of British decision-making, are relatively weak in defence against policies for which there is strong public support. Because Britain has a cabinet government and two tightly disciplined, oligarchical mass parties, there just was no channel through which the medical profession could apply successful pressure against socialized medicine other than through the Ministers themselves. Moreover, in the case of the National Health Service constitutional attitudes demanded the speedy implementation of the Labour Party's proposal; a clear mandate had been given. Perhaps this factor is not as important in this case as the concentration of decision-making power in British government and the power of the parties to 'integrate' interests, for it is the structure of decision-making which gives practical significance to the constitutional attitudes: after all, in the United States a 'mandate' for compulsory health insurance was given in 1948 and no legislation followed, this despite the fact that the myth of the mandate is more deeply established in the United States than in Britain. However, we need not weigh the operational significance of governmental structure and constitutional attitudes in this case, for the two factors clearly reinforce one another.

Even in the case of the National Health Service, however, a full explanation of the BMA's setbacks requires a more complicated explanation. Remember that the BMA's aims regarding the Service were not exclusively defensive. It did want delay, but more than that, it wanted an act which it had helped to draft. Remember also that mandate theory in Britain exists alongside other, sometimes contradictory, constitutional attitudes. If modern democratic attitudes demand that the general will prevail, older corporatistic notions demand that voluntary organizations have a voice in public determinations concerning the deepest interest of their members. Were genuine negotiations between the Minister and the negotiating committees really quite unthinkable in 1945 and 1946? Obviously not. Then what induced and enabled the Minister to resist them? And what made it possible for him to avoid the consequences threatened by the BMA in its anger over being ignored in the drafting of legislation?

A fully satisfactory explanation of the BMA's political setbacks must add three factors to the basic determinants already mentioned. One involves both the pattern of policy and the interdepartmental power structure. In 1945 and 1946 Labour had an enormous amount of parliamentary business to transact—not only its large legislative programme, but a great load of parliamentary work that had accumulated during the war, the re-shaping of war legislation to the purposes of peace, and the usual burden of routine and recurrent parliamentary business; an extensive welfare state was being created, and in this process parliamentary time had to be managed carefully and parsimoniously by a powerful cabinet committee, acting in light of departmental representations and general cabinet guide-lines. Bevan's power, although greater than that of subsequent Ministers, was hardly great enough to allow him to draw a blank cheque on parliamentary time, while the legislative projects of other Ministers were being brutally suppressed by Morrison's committee ('the slaughter of the innocents', as Morrison himself has called it); hence Bevan's freedom to negotiate with the profession was severely restricted by considerations too broad for the decision of an individual departmental minister. Secondly, it is clear that the internal structure of the medical profession, no less than the internal structure of the British executive, has played an important role in the BMA's setbacks. In 1912 the BMA was unable to sabotage the health insurance scheme chiefly because it turned out to have little control over individual doctors in a crisis; even before the BMA had called for the working of the scheme most British doctors had joined the health insurance panels and the conversion of the BMA's leaders at the eleventh hour merely ratified what had already happened without their guidance. So during the National Health Service negotiations it was the inability of the BMA to carry an important element of the profession, the more eminent specialists, which averted serious trouble; note the successful conciliation by the Presidents of the Royal Colleges at the most critical moment of the negotiations. Finally, to constitutional attitudes must be added attitudes within the medical profession which tend to weaken the Association in certain kinds of negotiations, especially the profession's aversion to overt trade union activities in general and organized strikes in particular. The fact is that the Government has never seemed to take seriously, or needed to take seriously, the more militant poses assumed by the Association. The desertion of individual practitioners to the health insurance panels in 1912 may be equated with the very lukewarm support of the Health Service defence fund in 1946 (only a small number of doctors contributed, and very little money at that); nor have threats to strike ever been allowed to mature on other occasions, such as during negotiations over doctors' pay both under national health insurance and the National Health Service.

The internal structure of the BMA, interdepartmental politics and professional attitudes account not only for the setbacks suffered by the BMA on basic medical policy, but also for its only partial successes in disputes over remuneration. The Ministry has been relatively intractable in negotiations concerning pay not because it is miserly but because the Treasury has compelled it to be stubborn; in this area, due to the interdepartmental power structure, the Ministry's scope for adjustment during negotiations has been smaller than in any other—ironically, because in this area, above all others, the right of the profession to negotiate terms has been unconditionally conceded, even in a purely formal sense. On the BMA's side, the officials' freedom of manoeuvre has been equally limited by the rank and file, for this is the one issue in which the members take a sustained and intense interest and demand adherence to the resolutions of their representative bodies. The result has always been impasse, bad feeling and recrimination—and inevitably so; both sides have longed for compulsory arbitration as a way out, the BMA openly, Ministry officials in private, but since such a step could remove remuneration from the Treasury's control it has not been possible to take it. In the disputes following deadlocks on pay the BMA has been severely hard put to mobilize a show of force in the classic trade union manner; threats to withdraw from the Service, campaigns to collect mass signatures from it for future use, attempts to build up large fighting funds have proved abortive and in the more serious disputes the Central Consultants and Specialists Committee has generally intervened to cool off the general practitioners, or to threaten them with an open split in case of drastic action. Ordinarily, therefore, internal divisions and normative inhibitions have prevented the BMA from breaking deadlocks over pay by unilateral force, while the relative weakness of the Ministry of Health has prevented it from securing important concessions for the profession at the political level; the result has usually been resort to arbitration after all, as the only alternative to deadlocks which neither side wants or is able to avoid.

Because of the BMA's internal structure its failure in matters regarding specialists need no further explanation, but it is still necessary to account for the Association's setbacks on proposals tending to improve and increase private practice. Only in this case need we go beyond the framework of determinants used throughout this study—policy, structure, and attitudes—to invoke a fourth determinant, administrative logic, although the factors previously mentioned play a role in this case too. Interdepartmental relations, for example, account for certain setbacks in this area because some of the BMA's proposals to improve the position of private practice would have increased charges on the exchequer (for example, a proposal to permit private patients to have prescriptions filled under the National Health Service)—and thus have brought into the picture the Treasury, at a time when general inflation and the unexpectedly high cost of the Service made economizing essential. Calculations of administrative feasibility, however, have played an equally important role.

Take, for example, the BMA's request that maximum limits be removed from the charges on pay-bed patients. Pay-beds in Health Service hospitals are supposed to serve a dual function: to provide special accommodation, usually in private rooms, to those willing to pay for them and to provide such accommodation to Health Service patients who need them on medical grounds. Patients who need the special facilities are supposed to get preference over patients who merely want them.[1] But few people were so naïve as to believe that specialists would keep their fee-paying customers out of the pay-beds in favour of Health Service patients. Removing limitations on fees which may be charged to pay-bed patients would only have aggravated a regrettable practice: encouraging patients to jump the queue for Health Service accommodation by using the pay-beds instead. I do not know how widespread this practice is, but it does exist and has been of concern to the Ministry.

One could argue, in short, that the whole set of purposes which the Health Service was meant to achieve—not only the provision of free services but also the broad regional planning of hospital facilities, central control over the distribution of general practitioners and the rationalization of general practice by encouraging various forms of group practice[2] —could be attained only by minimizing the scope of private practice: by preventing the growth of private nursing homes alongside the public hospitals and by inducing general practitioners to enter the service and thus to become subject to its controls and inducements. Thus we need not postulate that Ministers of Health and their officials have had a normative distaste for private practice to explain the BMA's setbacks in this area. What the BMA can achieve is limited, among the other factors mentioned, by what the Ministry can reasonably grant, just as the Ministry's scope of action is limited in many cases by what the profession can be made to accept; and even though it is not a narrowly constricting factor, the very logic of having to carry out certain policies limits the Ministry's ability to make concessions.

Achievements. The four basic factors which account for the BMA's failures also account for its achievements. Although they operate against the BMA in some areas and under certain circumstances, in most cases and under most conditions they operate in the Association's favour. We have seen that it is not the political weight of the BMA—its ability to mobilize public or parliamentary opinion or to swing doubtful constituencies—which explain its influence. What does explain it? Much of the answer we know from the previous chapter, for whatever promotes intimate relations between the Association and the Ministry

---

[1] *National Health Service Act,* 1946, Sec. 5, and *National Health Service (Pay-Bed Accommodation in Hospitals) Regulations,* S. I, 1948, No. 1490.

[2] For a discussion of the purposes which the Health Service was created to achieve, see Eckstein, *The English Health Service,* pp. 167–175.

also helps the Association to influence the Ministry's decisions. But at the risk of repetition let us review the more significant factors tending to give the BMA political power, in light of the considerations which tend to limit it and in light of the overall range of its achievements, weighing, in so far as one can weigh such things, the importance of these factors relative to one another.

Undoubtedly an important part of the explanation for the BMA's great political influence is to be found in the pattern of policy and the administrative requirements it poses, particularly the Ministry's need to win the positive co-operation of the BMA; such co-operation is needed for a great variety of reasons, from expert assistance to the use of the *British Medical Journal* for advertising vacancies in the public health and medical services. We need not retrace this argument, but we do need to qualify it; the dependence of public medical administration on the BMA's co-operation is important, but it is not alone sufficient to explain the BMA's striking influence at the Ministry. If the Association were really able to organize mass withdrawals from the Service, if it could really persuade doctors (as some members have wanted) to refuse to sign certificates required under the insurance and compensation acts (and thus make it impossible to administer these acts), if it could in fact prevail upon eminent specialists not to serve on Health Service advisory bodies or keep doctors from serving on the Health Service boards and committees, then we would not need to search further for reasons explaining its political effectiveness, but its influence over the profession has never been so great as all that.

Smooth and close relations between the Ministry and the Association are a matter of great convenience for both sides, but they do not exist just for that reason. To understand why they do exist it is essential to add two things: that, for structural reasons, it is *possible* for them to exist, and that, because of certain attitudes, it is both possible and *necessary* for them to exist.

It is important to bear in mind that the Ministry is in fact normally in a position to deal with the BMA free of the limitations of the inter-departmental power structure, an indispensable prerequisite, as we have seen, to large-scale concessions through negotiations. The concentration of decision-making powers in British government may act as an obstacle to the BMA in certain cases; usually, however, it is a positive advantage. When is it an obstacle? When the level of policy-making is the cabinet and parliament, when large political and interdepartmental calculations are made. When is it an advantage? When the Ministry is left a really free hand, as it can be only under a system like the British cabinet system. This explains why the Association managed to determine the shape of the Health Service Act through the Regulations when it had been denied the right to do so through the statute. As soon as the Act had been passed, the basic political deterrent to BMA influence—the mandate—ceased to operate; so also did the basic interdepartmental deterrent: the problem of apportioning parliamentary time. Out of the parliamentary limelight and free of his colleagues' pressures, the Minister could embark on leisurely and thorough negotiations, and through them rewrite the statute, not of course in any fundamental way, but to a very important extent. The Health Service Act had provided for a free and comprehensive medical service, but indicated only the bare outlines of its administrative structure; in most cases, therefore, positions subsequently negotiated with the BMA do not appear as outright revisions of the Act, but as elaborations of it. But we certainly have reason to think that in some cases (e.g. general practitioners' remuneration) the positions ultimately arrived at were very different from what was initially intended and that in others (e.g. Health Centres) provisions of the Act were actually rendered inoperative by the way it was implemented. What emerged was not a Service modelled upon the BMA's image of what it ought to be, but one much more affected by BMA attitudes than might have been supposed in the days when Bevan, supported by his party's unusually strong mandate, was treating the Association in a cavalier fashion.

That negotiations could shape the Health Service as much as they did must be attributed most fundamentally, of course, to the fact that much British legislation tends to be extremely vague and general, leaving even essential details to departmental regulations. This approach to legislation rests on certain basic constitutional attitudes, but depends also upon the existence of a certain structure of government: the correspondence and integration of legislature and executive. In other respects, attitudes have aided the BMA more independently of structure. That the Ministry was given a relatively free hand over medical policy after 1946 is attributable also to the lack of public and party-political concern with such policy, and this in turn to existence of broad consensus throughout Britain (even in the medical profession) on its general character. Finally, intimate relations between the Ministry and the Association are in a sense demanded by corporatistic attitudes. There was much genuine indignation in Britain against Bevan's summary treatment of the BMA during the drafting of the National Health Service Act, indignation due to the prevalent belief that voluntary organizations in general have a 'right' to be consulted, and more than consulted, when the interests of their members are deeply affected, and reinforced in this case by the particular deference which the medical mysteries command from laymen—including the laymen who run the Ministry of Health. The very intimate relations between the Ministry's and Association's officials may be made possible by the British power structure, but that such relations actually exist, and that consultations are as thorough and intensive as they are, cannot be fully explained simply by showing that close relations are possible, or even in many cases convenient. One has the impression that highly intimate relations between the Ministry and the BMA exist basically because it has never occurred to Ministers or their officials that they might not exist: that the learned representatives of the profession's most important organization might be treated simply as supplicants and consultants. Thus a basic cultural pattern is reflected in BMA–Ministry relations, however greatly exaggerated it may be by administrative calculations, structural relations, and a complex of other attitudes, all of which reinforce the BMA's power.

A final word about the role of structure in determining the BMA's influence at the Ministry. We have seen that the power of both parties—the Ministry's power of making final decisions on important subjects, the power of the BMA's leaders in acting as a liaison with the profession and helping in the administration of medical policy—helps account for the scope of the Association's influence. So perhaps do their weaknesses. One of the more weighty considerations the Ministry of Health can exert when interdepartmental questions do arise is that it has the approval of the medical profession for, or its insistence upon, a certain action. On the other hand, the BMA's pretensions to organize and speak for the whole profession, above all its current drive to win the primary allegiance of the specialists, depends upon its ability to establish close, preferably bipartite, relations with the Ministry. Both the Ministry and the Association, therefore, are encouraged to establish the closest possible relations and to seek agreement wherever possible. In this search for agreement, however, it is the Ministry which acts under the greatest compulsion to make concessions, for the BMA can realize its ambitions to become a truly monolithic structure only by being a highly successful bargaining agent for the profession.

V

A Successful Negotiation

From some very broad generalizations about the operation of pressure
groups in general we have gradually moved to levels of greater concrete-
ness: a detailed analysis of the conditions under which the BMA acts in
politics and a still more detailed description of the scope, structure,
spirit and effectiveness of its political relations. In this chapter and the
next we shall take still another step from the abstract to the concrete, by
reconstructing in detail the history of two negotiations between the BMA
and the Ministry. One of these, the Registrar negotiations of 1950 to
1954 (perhaps they are not really over yet) shows the BMA at perhaps its
most effective; the other, the earlier negotiations about general practitioners' remuneration under the National Health Service, shows it in
much greater difficulties. Together, these histories illustrate not only the
machinery of negotiation but also the power factors governing their
outcome in particular cases.

Before going into the negotiations, however, a *caveat* is required.
Neither history describes the negotiations as concretely as one might
like. This is because it has been necessary to rely heavily in their con-
struction on public sources of information, the *British Medical Journal*
and the *Lancet*, Hansard, and the press—plus certain more intimate
details culled from interviews with officials who have been understandably reticent about going beyond the publicly available data. The
trouble with official sources in this case is, of course, that they present a
purely official view of the negotiations. They tell us much about formal
meetings but little about contacts 'on the backstairs'. They tell us that a
'negotiating committee' went to the Ministry, but nothing about the men
who actually spoke for it or whom they saw. They tell us that the
Ministry took such and such a line, but not whether it took it after
prodding from the Treasury or on its own initiative. We are restricted
willy-nilly to the visible, not always important, aspects of the negotiating
machinery, at least until the thaw which ultimately unfreezes more

H

intimate details of government even in Britain has set in—usually about a half century after the event. To get a fully accurate picture of specific Health Service negotiations one must read a great deal between the lines, but in light of the relations depicted in Chapter III that should not be difficult.

Background

For the sources of the Registrar dispute we must go back to the very beginning of the National Health Service. One of the innovations made under the Service was the classification of specialists and specialist-trainees into grades, according to length of training and professional achievements, partly for purposes of remuneration and partly to establish a regular career ladder for specialists. Prior to the Health Service no such career ladder had really existed. A specialist then was simply a doctor who practised a speciality, and a 'consultant' a doctor who managed to have himself recognized as such; no clearly defined and formally enforced academic criteria had to be satisfied in either case. To be sure, specialists and consultants generally were doctors who had passed the examinations of the Royal Colleges and who held honorary appointments in the voluntary hospitals, both requiring considerably more than the ordinary medical training. But this was by no means universally the case. Plenty of specialists and hospital honoraries had dubious academic qualifications for their positions, and one of the purposes of the National Health Service was gradually to change this state of affairs by providing a hierarchy of grades through which specialists working in hospitals and providing domiciliary consultations had to move before they could qualify as full-fledged 'consultants'. After consultations with a Joint Committee of the Royal Colleges, the Scottish Royal Corporations and the BMA's Central Consultants and Specialists Committee, the following grades were created:[1] *Consultant* (the highest attainable grade, usually achieved at age 32 or over); (b) *Senior Hospital Medical Officer* (a grade envisaged at the outset partly as a temporary grade to absorb certain catagories of specialists from the pre-NHS hospital system, but which has become a sort of junior consultantship, also attained around the age of 30); (c) *Registrar* and *Senior Registrar* (envisaged as grades for younger men already highly trained, engaged part-time in still higher training, and part-time in research, hospital practices and teaching), (d) *House Officer*, *Senior House Officer* and *Junior Hospital Medical Officer* (grades for the first four years, approximately, of hospital training).[2]

At first it was intended that all grades below the very highest should

[1] Published in March 1949; accepted by the profession in July.
[2] See Ross, *National Health Service in Great Britain*, p. 152.

be 'training' grades pure and simple, that is, steps along which would-be specialists would progress in the course of their education, academic selection reducing the number of successful candidates at each level. Most of the unsuccessful trainees were to be forced into general practice. To make sense of the Registrar dispute, however, we must realize that this idea was not carried out from the very outset of the Service, and for a very good reason. To fit the Health Service grades to specialists already employed in the hospitals, a number of professional assessment teams were constituted to evaluate the specialists' qualifications in terms of the new categories. Immediately these teams ran into a difficult problem: what to do with inadequately qualified specialists, men often well advanced in years, employed in many of the lesser, and some not so minor, hospitals. They could not easily be forced into general practice at this stage of their careers; that would not have been kind to them, nor could many hospitals have carried on efficiently without them. It was hardly possible to treat them as trainees either, since many had attained the maximum skill of which they were capable. Nor was it possible to grade them as full-fledged consultants without making a travesty of the meaning of that category under the new dispensation. Almost all the assessment teams arrived at a solution which seemed logical at the time but helped to make a great deal of trouble later. They recommended, usually successfully, that most of the doubtful cases should be classified as Senior Hospital Medical Officers (or Senior Registrars) but not regarded as being in training; in short, that appointments for such doctors should be something in the nature of inferior consultantships, to be held indefinitely.

That was one of the crucial factors underlying the dispute which developed later. A second important cause of it was the Ministry's over-optimistic conception of the development of hospital and specialist services under the National Health Service. These conceptions, as it turned out were very far off the mark. A great expansion of hospital facilities was envisaged; little has taken place, and not a single new hospital has yet been built (1958) since the war. An even greater expansion of specialist services was envisaged. A remarkable pamphlet on the subject published by the Ministry of Health in 1950, the very year the Registrar dispute broke out (but prepared two years earlier) gives us a vivid picture of just what was expected to be attained; it makes very depressing reading in light of what has actually been achieved since then.[1] We need not go into the reasons for these discrepancies between

[1] Ministry of Health, *National Health Service: The Development of Consultant Services*, London, HMSO, 1950. First circulated as a memorandum to Regional Hospital Boards in 1948, but not revised in any important sense for publication in 1950.

aims and achievements here, but anyone acquainted with Britain's post-war economic situation will realize that there are many good ones and that the stagnation of the hospital service cannot be entirely attributed to the Ministry. The important point here is simply that appointments to specialist-trainee grades were made at first with confident expectations of a greatly expanded hospital service. Large numbers of young doctors, especially doctors returned from military service, were encouraged to enter training in hospitals as specialists—not that much encouragement was needed, for under modern conditions specialization has almost every advantage over general practice. Prospects of a multitude of new consultantships were dangled before the eager young men who met the intellectual requirements, while lesser lights established themselves in general practices. The immediate result was a vastly swollen junior specialist establishment, composed simultaneously of younger men still in training and older men who seemed to be settled for life. By November of 1950 there were 2,800 Registrars and Senior Registrars in the Service, not to mention SHMOs.

It is to the credit of the BMA's leaders—in view of subsequent events—that they saw from the beginning that something was wrong with this inflation of the lower specialist grades. Complaints were published in the *British Medical Journal* against the Ministry's policy of making apparently permanent appointments to these grades, and against the policy of turning younger men away from general practice into hospital positions.[1] Perhaps the BMA held this position for the wrong reasons: not because it foresaw the doldrums that would beset the hospital services but because of its bias in favour of general practice. Still, it held the right position.

About the beginning of 1950, officials of the Ministry of Health also began to realize that they had committed a serious blunder. The brave new hospital and specialist service just was not coming into being. Vacancies for would-be consultants were few and applicants distressingly many. Highly qualified men were unable to advance; the Registrar establishments were becoming stagnant; able young doctors faced the imminent threat of being forced into general practice by the lack of appointments above the JHMO level. Not only that, but the maintenance of the inflated Registrar establishments to staff non-existent facilities was proving an expensive luxury at the very time the Health Service was under severe fire for proving much more costly than had been forecast. Clearly it was necessary to do something about the hordes of redundant Registrars if a career ladder for specialists was indeed to be achieved.

Having decided upon action, Ministry officials moved with rather unusual speed. Apparently two meetings on proposed action were held

[1] See, e.g. *British Medical Journal*, 1950, I, 530.

in 1950 with representatives of the Joint Committee for Specialists; at these tentative approval of the Ministry's plans seems to have been given.[1] Why it was given, in view of the subsequent storm, it is very difficult to say. One may suspect that the eminent and solidly established specialists consulted by the Ministry were hardly aware of (or concerned about) the impact its proposals would have on the lesser specialists and opinion in the profession at large; if this is so, one can also understand why the initiative in opposing the Ministry's proposals soon passed, in fact if not in form, from the specialist corporations to the BMA. What precisely were the Ministry's proposals? They were stated in a memorandum circulated in November 1950.[2] Places could be found in the near future for only 1,700 new consultants at the rate of 150 annually: the Registrar grade was from now on to be purely a training grade and therefore to be limited in accordance with the probable number of higher openings; Registrars were to hold their posts for only two years and Senior Registrars for three, save only in very exceptional cases; *ergo*, from now on only 600 Senior Registrars and 1,100 Registrars could hold appointments. Corresponding quotas were fixed for the hospital regions, and the regional authorities were instructed to discontinue appointments as soon as possible to achieve their quotas. To help the Boards over short-run staff problems, a few temporary appointments were to be given to discontinued Registrars and a good many part-time hospital appointments to general practitioners. Finally, the memorandum pointed out to the one thousand odd redundant Registrars the attractions of service in the armed forces, the colonies and other areas overseas, in most of which terms of service were much worse than under the National Health Service.[3]

The Negotiations

The BMA's leaders and officials reacted to the Ministry's memorandum with great indignation, under the desperate prodding of the threatened Registrars acting through the BMA's own Registrars Group. The Ministry, according to a leader in the Journal, had 'gulled the public and beguiled the medical profession';[4] it was guilty of a breach of faith with the young doctors whom it had encouraged to specialize; most of those affected were doctors who might by now be solidly established in general practice instead of being compelled to start their careers all over again under much more difficult conditions. The issue was also brought up in Parliament by Dr Charles Hill, the former Secretary of the BMA.

---

[1] 'Seems', because the Joint Committee later denied that it had given its approval.
[2] Min. of Health Memo, RHB, 1950, No. 106.
[3] *British Medical Journal*, 1950, II, Supp. 204–6.
[4] *British Medical Journal*, 1950, II, 1158.

On a motion to adjourn, the subject was debated in the House of Commons on November 22, 1950, the Government not deigning to reply to its critics, perhaps because it realized that it had an unpopular case—unpopular not only because innocent doctors were now asked to suffer the consequences of faulty planning, or because most of these unfortunate men were ex-Servicemen, but also because the Registrars decision was a tacit admission of the failure of the Health Service to achieve some of its original objectives. The clamour against the memorandum was joined even by the Socialist Medical Association, despite its affiliation with the Labour Party[1] and, not long after, by members of the Joint Consultants Committee (including representatives of the Royal Colleges), whom the Ministry had originally consulted. The occasion for this falling out between the Ministry and the Royal Colleges was a parliamentary question raised on November 30th, asking the Minister whether he had consulted the profession on his proposals. Bevan replied that the new Registrar establishments had, in fact, been 'worked out' with the Joint Committee, but the Joint Committee quickly denied that it had agreed to the specific figures published;[2] from this point on the more eminent specialists seemed solidly opposed to the Ministry's plans along with the rest of the profession, making common cause with the Registrars Group of the BMA.

On December 15th the issue was again debated in the House of Commons on a motion to adjourn for Christmas put by Sir Hugh Lucas-Tooth and Mr (now Sir) Fred Messer, both MPs long interested in medical affairs. Bevan this time did offer a defence, arguing (a) that no one had ever *promised* a substantial development of consultant services (it had merely been envisaged), (b) that he was only trying to avoid future trouble by at last relating Registrar establishments to anticipated vacancies on the higher levels (a very strong argument), and (c) that the BMA was merely a trouble-making sectional interest opposed to a decision which was clearly in the general public's (financial?) interest. But in a manner characteristic of Bevan, British balm soon followed his Gaelic barbs: he would not close the doors upon future discussions of the issue, both with Regional Hospital Boards and representatives of the profession.[3] As it turned out, this was a tacit offer to suspend the memorandum pending wider consultations with the profession.

The first successful pressure on the Ministry, then, was brought to bear in Parliament by 'interested' and 'friendly' MPs. In the meantime, however, the profession itself was mobilizing for action. Regional Registrars' Associations held meeting after meeting; so did the Registrars

---

[1] *British Medical Journal*, 1950, II, 1372.
[2] *British Medical Journal*, 1950, II, Supp. 225.
[3] 482 H. C. Deb. 1526–47.

Group of the BMA.[1] On December 6th an emergency meeting of the Central Consultants and Specialists Committee was held at BMA House; about the same time the Joint Committee also met. The result was a joint request by the Joint Committee and the CCSC asking explicitly for deferment of the circular pending further discussions.

These discussions were re-opened on January 16, 1951, when the Sub-committee on Registrars of the Joint Committee went to discuss the circular with Ministry of Health officials. The discussions focused on a counter-memorandum prepared by members of the sub-committee, asking (a) that Registrar establishments should not be fixed until the plans of the Regional Boards for providing comprehensive specialist services (then still being prepared) were published, (b) that Registrars should not be treated as if they were merely trainees, but recognized as essential members of hospital medical teams (implying that their appointments should not be formally limited), (c) that Senior Registrar establishments should not be reduced quite so much and the proposed three-year term regarded as a minimum, not a maximum, and (d) that Registrar establishments should not be centrally limited at all but determined by the hospitals in terms of the medical services they provide. In making these proposals the sub-committee clearly had in mind not only the interests of younger Registrars but also those of middle-aged Registrars who could no longer hope to compete successfully for higher positions and many of whom were threatened with being forced into general practice, to start all over, late in their careers, work for which they were probably by now totally unsuited. Many of the Registrars actually threatened by dismissal were 35 or more years old, some with seven years or more of hospital training.

The discussions immediately resulted in important concessions. An 'agreed statement' was issued pointing out that the Ministry regarded the figures allowable in its memorandum only as 'target figures'; that these figures were far from 'inflexible' and to be revised in light of representations by the Regional Hospital Boards and the results of special staff surveys; that dismissals were in no case to be 'immediate' but spaced over at least twelve months; that no one would be dismissed whose services were needed (so much for the plan to fill the gaps by appointing general practitioners); and that regional allocations were also to be modified.[2] The profession had now achieved its first objective: to get the Ministry to go back on the definitive tone of its memorandum and to delay its implementation while discussions proceeded. A calmer atmosphere now existed, and for several months Ministry officials and

[1] See, e.g. the report of a meeting of the Council of the Registrars Group of the BMA, published in the *British Medical Journal*, 1951, I, Supp. 17–18.
[2] *British Medical Journal*, 1951, I, Supp. 24–5.

professional representatives negotiated quietly the new principles to govern junior hospital medical staffs, while most of the threatened Registrars remained uncertain of their ultimate fate.

In April of 1952 the Council of the BMA reported progress to the Association. The Ministry had made important concessions on almost every disputed point: Senior Registrar establishments would now be fixed at 960 instead of the 600 originally proposed, the normal term of appointment would be four instead of three years, and no central limitation state would be put on Registrar establishments.[1] Nevertheless, a sizeable number of Senior Registrars were still to be dismissed from their positions and the profession was still restive. Now, however, pressure shifted from the general principles of the Ministry's memorandum to its impact in concrete cases. Much was made of the problems of Registrars who had been wrongly graded, the lead being taken by the BMA's Central Consultants and Specialists Committee—which seemed, not surprisingly perhaps, much more concerned over their fate than the representatives of the Royal Colleges. The BMA's spokesmen conceded that it might be wise to appoint new Registrars only in light of vacancies reasonably expected on the higher levels, but, they argued, the Government had a moral responsibility toward specialists already under contract, especially those with long hospital careers behind them and graded as Registrars solely for the sake of convenience, or because no one had clearly understood when specialists were graded what qualifications would be required of Senior Hospital Medical Officers.[2] At the same time, the profession's representatives tried to obtain from the Ministry a promise that shortages of staff arising from reductions in the Registrar grades would be filled by appointing full-fledged consultants rather than by makeshift appointments.[3]

Representatives of the Joint Committee now were called in by Ministry officials to decide what was to be done about the 200 to 400 Senior Registrars (estimates varied) still to be dismissed. At the same time (about May 1st) the Council of the Registrars Group of the BMA asked that all Senior Registrars who had the ability to become consultants should be allowed to have their appointments renewed until appointments for them could be found—just what might have been expected from a group of predominantly young practitioners; the Registrars Group did not seem greatly concerned about the middle-aged Registrars, but broader public opinion within the Association was very

[1] 'Report of the Council', *British Medical Journal*, 1952, I, Supp. 164.
[2] See the Report of a meeting of the CCSC, held on Feb. 7, 1952, in *British Medical Journal*, 1952, I, Supp. 65–6.
[3] See the letter from the Chairman of the Registrar Group, *British Medical Journal*, 1952, I, Supp. 145.

concerned indeed, partly one supposes for reasons of Christian kindness, partly because the powerful general practitioners' section of the Association did not welcome the shift to general practice of many of the redundant Registrars. Under this further pressure the Chief Medical Officer of the Ministry of Health[1] sent a letter to the Joint Committee (about mid-May) making still more concessions: (1) in certain difficult specialties (neurosurgery, thoracic surgery, etc.) the reduction of Registrar establishments would be very gradual (although in other specialties much faster); (2) in fields in which prolonged training was desirable, Senior Registrars could be appointed for a *fifth* year; (3) Senior Registrars would be kept on a year to year basis in other cases where hospitals clearly needed their services. But that, said the CMO, was final. It was too bad about the older Registrars, but younger men should not indefinitely find their paths clogged by senior men who would sooner or later have to go anyway, and the redundant Registrars should not live in a fool's paradise but, in their own interest, start their careers anew as soon as possible. So there was nothing more to be said; all that could be done for the Registrars had been done.

The BMA's Central Consultant and Specialists Committee, however, was not satisfied even yet. In a meeting held on October 30, 1952, it decided to ask the Joint Committee to press for a general showdown on all dismissals—it was now two years since the original decision had been announced, and no one had been dismissed yet!—in the hope that time would smooth over everything. The meeting was reassured by a BMA official that the Ministry was at last taking the issue 'seriously' and was now 'willing to investigate it' with the Joint Committee! However, the Ministry seemed to regard the matter as closed and began putting Registrars 'under notice' in many areas.[2] Anguished calls for help now went out to BMA officials and representative bodies; the Joint Committee was prevailed upon to make fresh representations to the Ministry about Senior Registrars under notice for whom no alternative employment was available immediately. And the Ministry easily let itself be pushed once again into delaying action; to the representations of the Joint Committee it replied that it was now collecting figures from the Regional Hospital Boards to determine the exact extent of the problem and that it would not act until these figures had been compiled. That was in March of 1953. In April the Ministry's investigations were completed and negotiations were resumed. The concessions announced

[1] The Ministry really has two top officials. One is the Permanent Secretary, a layman as in other Ministries. The other, the Chief Medical Officer, who is mainly concerned with the supervision of environmental services and medical statistics, is a doctor. The CMO is sometimes employed, however, to take the lead for the lay officials in making conciliatory gestures toward the profession.

[2] *British Medical Journal*, 1953, I, Supp. 156.

by the CMO almost a year earlier as the end of the whole affair had proved to be merely a phase of it after all.

What line did the profession's representatives take now that the Ministry had all but withdrawn its original decision? The Registrars Group of the BMA still took a rather egocentric position; the 300 Senior Registrars actively put under notice should be dismissed but allowed to compete openly for other posts in their speciality against younger men and to be re-appointed, if qualified, for a further two years. The Joint Committee, however, was prevailed upon to take a more liberal line. It now argued that serious problems would arise in the hospitals if the dismissals actually took place, and it suggested—to make a good of a bad thing—that, since many of the Registrars under notice were doing Consultants' work anyhow, the ultimate solution lay in reducing Registrar establishments and increasing the number of higher-post consultants in compensation. This was hardly what the Treasury would have wanted, but, the Committee reported, Ministry of Health officials had received the proposal 'sympathetically'.[1]

A month later the Council of the BMA was able to report still further progress. The Ministry had agreed that Senior Registrars under notice could be retained by Regional Hospital Boards *until the end of 1955* wherever extra staff would have to be employed as the result of a dismissal; even then, dismissed Senior Registrars would be allowed to compete for other Senior Registrar appointments and to hold such appointments a further two years, so that for some the day of reckoning might be postponed until 1957. Can one wonder that the BMA crowed? 'The statement of agreement between the Minister of Health and the Joint Consultants Committee on the subject of surplus senior registrars in England and Wales,' said a leader in the *British Medical Journal*, 'is good news. It is the outcome of considerable pressure upon an adamant (*sic*)—albeit sympathetic—Ministry by the Joint Consultants Committee ably backed by the Registrars. In fact, the measures now proposed are largely those of the Registrars Group of the BMA.'[2]

Yet even this is not the end of the story. Having pushed back the Ministry almost to the position prevailing before Memorandum RHB 1950 No. 106 was issued, the profession, looking ahead to the day when no further postponement of the dismissals would be possible, urged the Ministry all the more intensely to increase the number of consultants' posts, so that any excess in the Registrar establishments could be absorbed by promotions. This pressure was applied with special force in the fields of general medicine and surgery, where the smallest number of vacancies for consultants were available. At the same time, while looking

[1] *British Medical Journal*, 1953, I, 222.
[2] *British Medical Journal*, 1953, I, 1154.

increasingly to the long run, the profession continued to press also certain short-run aims. Regional Hospital Boards were prevailed upon to give redundant Registrars as broad experience as possible to enable them to choose among a variety of alternative careers. The Boards were also asked not to put dismissed Registrars at an unfair disadvantage when competing for appointments[1] and to take full advantage of the Ministry's new policy by extending Registrar appointments. But the bulk of the activities of the BMA in regard to the redundant Registrars after 1953 concerned negotiations over individual cases. In March 1954, the chairman of the Registrars Group asked every displaced Registrar who wished to have his case reviewed to contact him and present particulars; these individual cases were then discussed with Ministry officials and in some cases the reviews apparently succeeded in postponing action. Later in 1954 a final concession on a point of 'principle' was won: those Senior Registrars considered capable of promotion could now be retained 'indefinitely on a transitional basis'; only some of the originally misgraded specialists would have to go.

Evaluation

What was the final result? In the end, only about a hundred or so Registrars were actually dismissed, (compared with the 1,100 originally scheduled),[2] and a few more have drifted voluntarily out of the hospital service every year because they realized the ultimate hopelessness of their position. The principle that the Registrar grades are training grades has been reaffirmed, and establishments have been frozen at the 1955 level by agreement between the Ministry and the Joint Consultants Committee. On the whole, however, the situation is not very different from what it was at the beginning. The long-run problem, how to achieve a smooth flow of specialists from the lowest to the highest specialist grades with a minimum waste of talent, has not been solved at all; the immediate problem, what to do with surplus Registrars who have no chance to progress further, was, in most cases, merely put off. For these reasons we have surely not yet heard the last of the redundant Registrars; but for the moment the profession—especially the BMA's Central Consultants and Specialists Committee and its Registrars Group—has proved triumphant on every issue.

Why did the Ministry concede so much to the profession's representatives? It might be answered, because it had such a bad case to begin with; and so in some respects it did. Certainly the miscalculations and the misgrading which created the problem were the Ministry's responsi-

---

[1] *British Medical Journal*, 1954, I, Supp. 93.
[2] I have not been able to obtain absolutely precise information on this point, but all the figures mentioned by informants have been around 100.

bility. But two wrongs do not make a right, and in the ill-starred memorandum of 1950 the Ministry undoubtedly had a good, even if unpopular, case, as the specialists' initial agreement with it suggests. What, after all, has been the good of keeping on, year after year, inferior Registrars, without hope of promotion, clogging up the advance of more talented younger men? Who should be forced out of the hospital service, the less talented or the more talented? Nor was the problem posed solely by the misgraded Registrars, those with little hope of advancement. In the final analysis, the problem arose chiefly because of what had become known about the future of the hospital service in 1950 that was not known about it before: that it would expand only slightly, if at all, in the foreseeable future. The crucial fact is that every consultant, during his tenure of office, trains from five to six Registrars, and that there must consequently be some considerable waste of talent at the higher training grades, short of a constant and enormous expansion of the specialist services. Even if Registrar establishments had been frozen in 1955—if no new Registrar establishment had been appointed sub-sequently—it would have taken eight years to absorb the existing establishment in general surgery to consultantships, ten years in general medicine, nine in obstetrics and gynaecology, eleven in orthopaedic surgery, and so on. The merit of the Ministry's case was that it attempted to achieve ruthlessly an end desirable both to itself and the BMA (the constant flow and displacement of would-be consultants) which can be achieved only by ruthless action of one sort or another, now or in the future.

Undoubtedly, Ministry officials realized this all along. That they gave in nevertheless to the profession's much more short-sighted views must be attributed either to bad conscience or irresistible pressure. And indeed the pressure brought to bear upon the Ministry was enormous. Pressure was brought to bear through Parliament; it was exerted by the Regional Hospital Boards; above all, it came from every professional body concerned with the problem: the Joint Consultants Committee, the Central Consultants and Specialists Committee, the BMA Council and Representative Body, the Registrars Group, the BMA Secretariat, and the Regional Registrars Associations. Professional ranks were hardly ever broken after the first BMA salvo against the memorandum of 1950 was fired. We can discern different professional interests behind some of the suggestions made: the interest of general practitioners in having a large number of potential competitors employed in other capacities, or the interest of members of the Registrars Group in having the Registrar grades treated purely as temporary training grades. Generally, however, younger and older practitioners, specialists and general practitioners, even socialist and non-socialist doctors, presented a united front. On the other side of the bargaining table the Ministry got little reinforcement from other departments. The issue was not of great political importance or, after the first publicity given to the memorandum, of great public concern. It was treated as a matter between the Ministry and the profession, even by the Treasury, for which the financial stakes involved were picayune, particularly after the storm over the supplementary estimates needed to run the Health Service in 1949 and 1950 had blown itself out. Under these circumstances, the powers of the profession were at their maximum, those of the Ministry at their minimum, and the final result (if indeed the result is final) just what might have been expected.

VI

An Unsuccessful Negotiation

THE STRUGGLE OVER SPENS

1948-1951

Although relations between the Ministry and the BMA were close and conciliatory from the outset of the National Health Service, one area of negotiation acted constantly as an irritant: the remuneration of general practitioners. The early years of the Service were marred by endless conflicts on the subject, from friendly criticism on points of detail to the most acrimonious disputes over points of principle. Nor do these conflicts seem to be abating now. If anything, they have become steadily more virulent. I shall deal here only with the disputes from 1948 to 1952, from the Spens Report to the Danckwerts award, but the story could be carried forward, if space permitted and if any new light could be shed on BMA–Ministry relations by doing so, up to this very moment.

Disputes over general practitioner remuneration which cannot be resolved by easy accommodation among the principal parties seem to be inherent in the National Health Service. Remuneration is the one subject on which the BMA's leaders seem unable to control pressure from the rank and file and the one subject on which the Ministry's freedom of action is sure to be restricted by powerful extra-departmental pressures. Caught between these forces, which always remain in the background as inexorable pressures, representatives of the Ministry and profession engage in perpetual sparring sessions, until conflict reaches such a pitch that outside parties—now a special arbitrator, now the Presidents of the Royal Colleges, now the Prime Minister—have to be brought in to bring about a temporary settlement. It is widely believed in Britain that for this an imperfect machinery of negotiation is responsible, but it is difficult to see how any machinery could lessen the pressures on both sides which have in the past prevented easy agreements.

General Practitioner Remuneration in the Health Service
The system of remuneration of Health Service general practitioners had an auspicious beginning, despite the troubles it has generated. Its

provisions were recommended in outline by an impartial committee of experts, the Spens Committee, whose recommendations both the Ministry and the Association accepted with some enthusiasm.[1] Its details were negotiated and agreed upon through the usual channels, with apparent satisfaction to both sides.[2] Only the issue of the basic salary created any important conflict, and on this, as we have seen, the Minister backed down stage by stage until he had granted all of the profession's demands. It follows that good relations on the subject broke down as quickly as they did because of external forces; but before coming to that, we need to examine the system agreed upon by the BMA's and Ministry's negotiators over which all subsequent controversy has raged.

The Spens Committee was concerned with two aspects of the remuneration system, the level of incomes to be paid to general practitioners and the basic method of payment (whether by salary, capitation fees, or fee-for-service), leaving the finer details of the distribution system to be worked out by the Ministry. As a basis for its recommendations, it compiled figures on the pre-war incomes of general practitioners, and discovered that the majority were far lower than was generally supposed.[3] It then recommended that general practitioners as a group should receive a large raise over pre-war income and specified the net amounts to be earned by various proportions of them (in 1939 values): three-fourths were to earn at least £1,000 net a year, one-half over £1,300, one-fourth over £1,600, and about 10 per cent over £2,000.[4] These levels of income of course were to reflect the experience, effort and skill of practitioners, to reward the able and industrious and penalize the inefficient. It is not difficult to understand why these basic recommendations proved so palatable to the BMA. They were very generous.

But how were the recommended levels of income to be achieved? What method of payment would reward doctors in proportion to their skill and industry and achieve the distribution recommended by Spens into the bargain? Here we come to the first source of subsequent difficulties: the inability of the Spens Committee to make any definitive administrative proposals as to how its quantitative recommendations might be realized. The Committee understood well enough that the easiest method, paying salaries graduated according to experience and

[1] *Report of the Interdepartmental Committee on the Remuneration of General Practitioners*, HMSO, 1948.
[2] See *British Medical Journal*, 1948, II, Supp. 177.
[3] About a fourth of all general practitioners earned net incomes of less than £700 a year; another third had less than £1,000. Really high incomes (over £2,500) were earned by less than 3 per cent of general practitioners. See *Spens Report*, p. 4.
[4] *Ibid.*, p. 3.

professional achievement, would be totally unacceptable to the profession, because of a deeply ingrained prejudice against salaries, even high salaries. It therefore recommended, with considerable reticence, the capitation system used under National Health Insurance, chiefly on the ground that the system would be acceptable to the profession and, incidentally, in the belief that it offered a 'possible' means of securing income differentiations according to degrees of ability and effort—a highly dubious proposition, based on the prevalent superstition that the size of a doctor's list accurately reflects his professional capacities. The Committee did suggest that very able general practitioners should be provided additional incomes by being paid for the training of young general practitioners as assistants; but except for this, it was willing to let the logic of the capitation payment work out its detailed recommendations.

There have been no disputes between the Ministry and the Association about these broad recommendations, but there have been plenty of wrangles about the empirical question whether the recommendations have ever been realized or not. This question has raised incredibly complicated issues, chiefly because the Spens Committee bequeathed to the Ministry two problems which, in my opinion, defy solution: how to translate its figures into post-war values and how actually to distribute pay so as to realize the all too facile Spens recommendations. What is a fair post-war equivalent of pre-war values? The answer needs to be calculated not only in terms of changes in the general cost of living, but also in terms of changes of taxation, the workload of general practitioners, the economic position of other learned professions, the level of practice expenses (which need not reflect the general cost of living at all faithfully), and so on.[1] It is clear that the subject is complicated enough to enable anyone to arrive at practically any figure he likes. But the problem of finding equivalent values is child's play compared to the problem of distributing funds under the capitation system in accordance with the Spens proposals.

From the outset, everyone agreed that it would not be advisable to pay doctors flat capitation fees and nothing else. The basic system recommended by the Spens Committee had to be tinkered with, stretched here and limited there, not only because the size of doctors' lists need not perfectly reflect their abilities but because it need not even reflect the amount of work they do. Numerically identical lists simply do not necessarily require identical amounts of work; take the case of rural as compared with urban practices, industrial compared with suburban practices, or health resort practices (which involve a high

[1] For a fuller discussion of the relevant factors, see the *Economist*, June 18, 1951, and *Medical World*, vol. 74, pp. 483-4.

proportion of elderly and chronic patients) compared with all the rest. Because of these and similar problems, the distribution scheme and the types of payment additional to capitation charges ultimately agreed upon by the Ministry and the BMA were complicated almost to the point of being unfathomable.

It was finally decided that practitioners should receive the following payments in addition to capitation fees: (a) a basic salary of £300, if desired by the practitioner and granted by the Executive Council in consultation with the local Medical Committee; (b) payment for emergency treatment given to patients not on a doctor's list; (c) mileage payments where practitioners have to travel long distances to treat their patients, thus compensating for the greatest difficulty of rural practice; (d) payment for dispensing drugs and appliances directly to patients, also most common in rural practices; (e) special fees for providing maternity services and administering anaesthetics for another practitioner; (f) supervision fees for having assistants, if the practitioner is approved as a post-graduate teacher in general practice; (g) 'inducement payments' payable in areas unattractive to general practitioners (e.g. where population is sparse) as determined by the Minister after consultation with the Medical Practices Committee.[1]

These payments were to be distributed through an incredibly complex scheme, which, unfortunately, we cannot avoid sketching.[2] First, the Government calculated the income general practitioners would have had in 1939 under Spens scales and added a 20 per cent increase on net incomes as a monetary 'betterment' factor, a 55 per cent increase in practice expense, and a further 3 per cent increase to compensate for the growth in population. (In all, total incomes were increased about 50 per cent.) It then took 95 per cent of this total, equal to the population percentage likely to use the Service, and thus arrived at a Central Pool which, it thought, reflected the amount recommended by the Spens Committee in 1948 monetary terms. It added to this sum a further sum for mileage allowances, dispensing fees, training fees, inducement payments and 'fixed annual payments'. This gave it the total amount to be paid general practitioners for all purposes. (These calculations should be kept in mind, for they soon led to intense dispute.) The next step, after calculating the size of the central pool, was to subtract the money earmarked for mileage payments; the remainder was then divided, in proportion to patients, among England, Wales, and Scotland. At this point charges for temporary patients were taken out of the national

---

[1] *National Health Service (General Medical and Pharmaceutical Services) Regulations*, S. I, 1948, No. 506, First Schedule, part II.

[2] See Ministry of Health, *Handbook for General Practitioners*, 1950, which summarizes all the relevant statutory instruments and memoranda.

pools and the remainder distributed, again in proportion to patients, to the various Executive Councils. At this third level, basic salaries and fees for emergency treatment were subtracted from the local pools, and the remainder finally distributed to the doctors in proportion to the size of their lists. In brief, no fixed capitation fee was paid, the value of patients varying from one area to another since it depended on local subtractions from each pool.

Apart from the fact that the system did weight patients to some extent according to difficulty of practice and that it gave a very small number of practitioners a cushy supplementary income as teachers of assistants, what had this system to recommend it? Only two things. It permitted exact advance calculations of the cost of the general practitioner service to be made every year despite the unpredictability of the number of patients, doctors, emergency treatments, etc.; but this would hardly recommend the system to anyone but the Treasury. Secondly, it was acceptable to the profession, at any rate at the outset (and very surprisingly too). But, on the other hand, the system raised a host of problems. For example, as earlier pointed out, it set unestablished and established practitioners at odds, since special payments to men with small lists came almost directly out of the pockets of those with larger lists;[1] it thus threatened to impede the geographic redistribution of general practitioners. It also encouraged doctors to take on large lists of patients, by making income proportionate—except for the fixed annual payment—to size of list; apart from the possibility that the result might be slip-shod practice, this also would tend to inhibit the redistribution of practitioners by making it more difficult for new doctors to build up profitable practices. (Many people, at any rate, believed that it would be far more sensible from every standpoint to weight the volume of patients so as to give doctors with small lists relatively larger incomes by decreasing on a sliding scale the marginal value of patients.) Finally, the system raised still another, and even more serious problem: what logical relation could there be between the results of the distribution scheme adopted and the agreed intentions of the Spens Committee?

In essence, the system of remuneration which was agreed upon by the Ministry and the Association stirred up conflict over two sets of interests. On one hand, conflict was generated over the vested interest of the established profession in the overall size of the pool and in the protection of its practices against competitive intruders. On the other hand, conflict arose over the vested interest of the Ministry in keeping charges on the Exchequer to a 'realistic' level and achieving a not too gradual redistribution of medical manpower. These conflicts became the

[1] See above, p. 68.

themes of all the troubles that followed. Was the central pool big enough, and was it distributed in a manner conducive to the broader purposes of the Service?

The Definition of the Issues, 1948–49

We have noted that the BMA's spokesmen had agreed to the system of remuneration adopted in 1948, once the objectionable feature of the universal basic salary had been dropped. But the spokesmen had, as usual, spoken mainly for themselves and pressure from the ranks of the general practitioners soon broke down the harmony which Bevan had established by his strategic concessions on the issue of salaries. One of the most striking aspects of the early negotiations over remuneration is this very lack of rapport between leaders and followers in the Association, a lack of rapport existing latently as the normal thing but made manifest in this case because of the deep interest of ordinary doctors in their incomes.

Even on the issue of basic salaries the leadership was clearly out of tune with most of the membership. From the time of the Beveridge Report, the profession had concentrated official opposition to all proposals for socialized medicine on the issue of a salaried service. Such a service would 'chain the profession to Whitehall'; it would lead to interference by laymen in clinical relations; it would lower the standards of practice. The threat of salaries was a convenient peg on which to hang all arguments for delay and reconsideration, for most of the profession undoubtedly was deeply opposed to whole-time salaried service. By 1946, the BMA leaders had become so much convinced by their own propaganda about salaries that in discussions about general practitioner remuneration they seem to have talked about nothing else. That, perhaps, was their undoing. While wrestling concession after concession on the issue of basic salaries from an all too tractable Ministry, the BMA leaders had no constructive alternative suggestions to make, and when, finally, the Ministry had conceded the whole of the BMA's demands on the subject (by July 1948), it proved only too easy for its officials to press their own scheme for remuneration on the BMA spokesmen. The initiative had passed from the BMA to the Ministry, just because the Association's leaders had been contesting a phantom issue; and so the Ministry's distribution scheme was introduced while the BMA negotiators seemed paralysed by Bevan's ready concessions on a subject supposed to produce irreconcilable conflict.

The concentration of all official medical opposition on the issue of the basic salary turned out to be a serious tactical blunder. Their intense preoccupation with this subject somehow blinded the BMA's negotiators to the really important issue: the size of the 'central pool' to be distributed to general practitioners. The 'betterment factor' (that is, allowance for change in the cost of living and the level of professional incomes since 1939) used by the Ministry in calculating the pool was almost ludicrously low (see p. 129)—so low that one suspects it was originally intended merely as a basis for haggling. Had the BMA raised objections when the original calculations were announced it would undoubtedly have got a large increase; after all, the Ministry was very open-handed at the beginning of the Health Service. Instead, the gauntlet was thrown down only after the Association had silently endorsed the Ministry's calculations, and not until the Ministry's freedom to budget had been severely circumscribed by pressure from the public and the Treasury. It is difficult to account for this on any ground other than the BMA leaders' obsession with the basic salary.

Meanwhile, however, many members of the Association had diagnosed that it was more important to settle disputed details of remuneration than to indulge in lofty oratory about uncontested principles. For one thing, the rank and file, despite its opposition to whole-time salaried service, seemed much less disturbed than the leaders by the prospect of 'basic salaries'; indeed, around August of 1948 one gets a good deal of correspondence in the *British Medical Journal* in favour of larger basic salaries. But the real issues to the rank and file were how much money general practitioners were to get, and how exactly funds would be distributed among them: how much would be allocated to mileage allowances, how much to inducement payments, what were to be the maximum number of patients permitted on a list, and so on. Such concrete issues were the chief concern of the Annual Representative Meeting held in Cambridge in 1948 and of resolutions and memoranda drawn up by branches and divisions.[1]

Under pressure from the members, the interest of the BMA leaders shifted from broad principles to narrow statistical calculations, and responsibility for negotiations devolved from the highest levels of the leadership to the Remuneration Sub-committee of the General Medical Services Committee, a very powerful body despite its subordinate position; its Secretary then was Dr Derek P. Stevenson, who is now the Secretary of the whole Association. BMA pressure now gradually

---

[1] For the official concern with basic salaries, see *British Medical Journal*, 1948, I, 936 and 1948, II, Supp. 131; for criticisms of the BMA's conduct of the negotiations, *ibid.* 1948, II, 393 and 397 and 1949, I, Supp. 46–8, 52 and 89. Perhaps the most bitter memorandum against the leaders was drawn up by the Winchester Division. This memorandum criticized the manner in which the BMA Council is elected and openly charged that the headquarters staff was out of touch with the members. 'Members have been discouraged to find', it stated, 'that while they have been engaged in a battle of general principles—capitation fees versus salary, etc.—negotiations of which were were not fully informed appear to have been proceeding over terms and conditions of service.'

became concentrated on all subjects related to the actual size of doctors' incomes. To be precise, the Association now wanted a higher basic capitation fee, a higher mileage allowance for rural practitioners, a larger inducement fund for practitioners in unattractive areas, and retroactive payments for vaccinations and immunizations given by general practitioners (not initially paid for as 'abnormal' services). Finally, having long argued that the natural force of the capitation system would lead to the redistribution of doctors from over-doctored to under-doctored areas without any central control, it demanded that unlimited funds be made available to special 'hardship cases': primarily doctors practising in, and unwilling to leave, over-doctored areas whose incomes had been severely reduced under the capitation system.[1]

The BMA, in short, was now acting as a trade union, and as such it quickly gained some important concessions. During these early days, as I have said, the cost of the Health Service had not yet become an issue of intense public and interdepartmental concern and the Ministry could shift funds about or make unexpected additions to its budget with relative ease. For example, a deputation of the General Medical Services Committee went to see the Minister of Health on December 22, 1948, to argue the case of rural practitioners for larger mileage allowances. On January 14, 1949, the Ministry announced that it had increased the mileage fund from £1,300,000 to £2,000,000, by shifting some money out of the so-called special inducement fund (for unattractive areas) and adding half a million not previously budgeted at all. The BMA leaders smugly claimed in the *Journal* that this concession was 'a tribute to (their) pertinacity',[2] but clearly not much prodding was required to soften the Ministry on the subject.

These, however, were only preliminary skirmishes. While the profession was pressing for small concessions on the margins of the remuneration system it was also preparing a broader case for wholesale increases in the central pool and for certain changes in its distribution —while, on the side of the Government storm clouds were gathering over the request for supplementary estimates to meet the unexpectedly high cost of the Health Service. The all-important issue of the proper size of the 'betterment factor' to be used to convert 1939 figures into contemporary values was first raised in January 1949.[3] The Secretary of the BMA reported (rather artfully, I think) that the Association had not yet raised this issue because it had preferred to wait until official Whitley machinery had been established, but that delays in its organization made it necessary to press the subject now, through less official channels.[4] An

[1] *Ibid.*, 1948, II, Supp. 145–6, 203–7, 215–6, 235, and 1949, I, Supp. 48.
[2] *Ibid.*, 1949, I, 109.
[3] *Ibid.*, 1949, I, Supp. 55–57.
[4] *Ibid.*, 1949, I, Supp. 55–57.

'expert had already been appointed to prepare an index comparing the post-war cost of living of the professional classes with the pre-war cost'.[1] At the same time, the General Medical Services Committee embarked on a survey of how levels of incomes were actually distributed within the profession. The problem before the GMSC was not only whether the central pool was large enough, but whether the distribution of incomes recommended by the Spens Committee had actually been achieved under flat capitation payments or whether it could be attained only by paying special premiums for certain patients, e.g. the first thousand on a list.[2]

By February 9th, the GMSC had at last prepared the case to be presented to the Ministry for full-scale negotiations, and by April 2nd, almost a year after the Appointed Day, its case had been given formal sanction by a special Conference of Representatives of Local Medical Committees and a Special Representative Meeting of the BMA. Both carried the GMSC's report with little cavilling and no important amendments. The Committee made two important proposals. First of all, it made certain suggestions as to what the size of the central pool should be in the light of the Spens Report, arriving at a figure a great deal larger than was being paid by the Ministry. Adding to the original Spens proposals allowances for a larger number of doctors and a larger population, it arrived at a base figure of £35·8 million, which, the Committee felt, should be increased by a betterment figure of 70 per cent, yielding a total central pool of £60 million; the actual central pool was then about £40 million.[3] The new figure, moreover, was to be retroactive to the Appointed Day. Secondly, the GMSC proposed that funds won by an increase in the betterment factor should be devoted entirely to higher capitation fees for the first 1,000 patients on doctors' lists (almost doubling their value), a recommendation which would benefit all doctors evenly, whether they had large lists or small, but which would, in the Committee's opinion, permit the disappearance of basic salaries and special inducement payments.

On these grounds, demanding much higher earnings all round and willing to permit the weighting of patients if this should lead to a

[1] For his report, see *ibid.*, 1949, I, Supp. 31.

[2] At first, the BMA leaders had regarded the 'weighting' of patients with great suspicion. The basic salary, for example, had been criticized in early negotiations because (among other things) 'it led to a tapering capitation fee position'. It was an 'illustration of a commercial practice of a penny each or three for twopence'. *Ibid.*, 1949, I, Supp. 21. By January 1949, however, they saw in it two advantages which affected a conversion: they believed that basic salaries, still a horrible bogy at BMA House, could be dispensed with altogether if patients were weighted, and they felt that by agreeing to such weighting they could squeeze more money out of the Ministry for the profession without having to get a flat increase in the capitation payment. *Ibid.*, 1949, I, Supp. 21.

[3] *Ibid.*, 1949, I, Supp. 67. See also Ross, *National Health Service in Great Britain*, p. 227.

decrease in non-capitation payments, the Association, led by its Secretary and the members of the GMSC's Remuneration Sub-committee, proposed to encounter the Ministry.

The Negotiations, 1949–50

On April 14, 1949, a rather large deputation of members of the GMSC, headed by the chairman, Dr S. Wand (now—1959—chairman of the BMA Council), saw officials of the Ministry to discuss these proposals—which, incidentally, had apparently been tendered to the Ministry some weeks before they were approved by the Conference of Local Medical Committees and the Special Representative Meeting![1] The Ministry's officials hedged; they suggested that discussion should be postponed until further inquiries had been made into the actual numbers of doctors in the Service and the actual incomes of practitioners. Perhaps this was reasonable enough, and the meeting might have broken up calmly had not a side issue of great importance been raised. Probably anticipating that a Ministry afflicted by criticism of the cost of the Health Service would be tough to deal with, the BMA representatives asked whether, in the event remuneration was dealt with by a Whitley Council, recourse could be had to arbitration in event of a disagreement. The Ministry hedged on this too: participation in the Whitley machinery could not be 'assumed' without further discussion to involve a right to compulsory arbitration. This the BMA representatives considered, with some justification, a 'breach of faith', in light of promises previously made.[2] They publicized the Ministry's position with many protestations of outrage; nor were they mollified by the provision of the Amendment Act introduced shortly afterwards which made disagreements about remuneration trade disputes under the Industrial Courts Act of 1919 and the Conciliation Act of 1896 (thus making it possible for the Minister of Labour to refer such disagreement to an Industrial Court for settlement with both parties' consent, or for 'advice', in the event consent were not given[3]). The BMA, correctly scenting trouble, wanted *compulsory* arbitration and nothing less.[4]

We should, of course, bear in mind here (and throughout the rest of the narrative) certain concurrent issues of financial planning and policy which affected the outcome of the negotiations regarding doctors' incomes. The initial meetings on the BMA's demands were held under circumstances which were bound to make both the Treasury and Ministry reluctant to grant concessions. In February of 1949, seven

[1] *British Medical Journal*, 1949, I, Supp. 237.
[2] *Ibid.*, 1949, I, 762, and Supp. 282–3; also 1949, II, 63.
[3] *National Health Service (Amendment) Act*, 1949, Section 13.
[4] *British Medical Journal*, 1949, II, Supp. 4–5.

months after the National Health Service had come into operation, the Minister of Health had been compelled to request a very large supplementary appropriation in order to pay for it—almost £53 million, or nearly 30 per cent of his original estimate. Many reasons account for this failure of the Minister and his officials to estimate the cost of the Service accurately, some unfavourable to them and others not. Of course, it was difficult to predict with accuracy the cost of a service for which so little previous experience was available, but the size of the supplementary estimate led to much unfavourable publicity and provided the opponents of the service with much cheap ammunition; it was widely interpreted to imply a combination of bad administration by the officials and abuse of the Service by patients. Nor does the Treasury like large supplementary estimates under any circumstances. These facts alone would have made the Ministry take a jaundiced view of the BMA's demand for a very large raise; but when one adds the fact that the Ministry's estimates for the next financial year were submitted to the House of Commons on March 1, 1949[1] (and, of course, prepared much earlier) it becomes apparent that the BMA's demands could not have been made at a more inauspicious time. We may be sure that the Ministry, being under pressure in regard to the overall cost of the Service, did not leave any scope in its estimates for 1949–50 for unexpected expenditures of the size envisaged by the BMA, and that concessions at this stage, whether negotiated or the result of arbitration, would surely have meant another supplementary estimate of considerable size, and a still more concerted attack on the Ministry and the Service. Hence the Ministry's hedging and obvious playing for time at this stage.

Disputes over the total amount of remuneration and the question of arbitration dragged on with much heat throughout the year. Meanwhile, however, the Association's leaders and the Ministry's officials, now bitterly at odds on some issues, were amicably negotiating and settling many other questions, including some involving remuneration. We should note this in order to put the more acrimonious (and more widely publicized) aspects of their relations in proper perspective. For example, important negotiations concerning the distribution of mileage funds took place in 1949 and 1950 between Ministry officials and the Rural Practitioners Sub-committee of the GMSC; these negotiations culminated in something close to total victory for the GMSC.[2] Important concessions were also won on the administration of special inducement funds and a number of minor matters.[3] Why was the Ministry so accommodating on

[1] 462 H. C. Deb. 192–5.
[2] See ibid., 1949, I, Supp. 288; 1949, II, Supp. 146 and 150; 1950, I, Supp. 137 and 279; and 1950, II, Supp. 37 and 100.
[3] Ibid., 1950, I, Supp. 110 and 229; and 1949, II, Supp. 135.

these subjects? Surely because they involved primarily adjustments within the distribution of the central pool rather than affecting the overall size of the pool, and thus were matters of concern to the Ministry alone and matters which did not threaten a need for supplementary supply. Had the Ministry enjoyed greater freedom in other negotiations their outcome might have been more favourable to the BMA too; but from the beginning of 1949 the shadow of the Treasury hovered inexorably over all discussions concerning the overall size of the central pool and compulsory arbitration. On the latter question, the Ministry simply could not give unilaterally (without the Treasury's consent) the guarantees demanded by the BMA even had it wanted to give them (all its pronouncements suggested that, *so far as it alone was concerned*, disputes over remuneration arising from the regular Whitley machinery, would be sufficiently arbitrable).[1] On questions regarding the size of the central pool its freedom was restricted even more severely, so that this issue quickly became the principal matter of dispute.

After the crucial meeting of April 14, 1949, the Ministry did embark on a survey of its own regarding the number of doctors in the Service, the distribution of incomes among them, changes in the volume of work and other factors bearing upon the proper size of the central pool. Its investigations were completed late in July and forwarded, together with the inferences which the Ministry drew from them, to the GMSC on August 18th, that is, just before the time when the Ministry begins planning the next year's estimates. The GMSC hired an eminent actuary to help it study the report and soon decided that, while it could agree to the facts found by the Ministry, it could not agree to its inferences regarding proper remuneration. It asked the Ministry to receive a delegation immediately to discuss the matter, but because the officials concerned had gone on vacation the meeting had to be postponed until September 23rd.[2] On that day, finally, a three-hour session took place between a deputation from the GMSC and Ministry officials, most of it devoted to criticism of the Ministry's figures. The Ministry agreed quite amicably to reconsider,[3] giving to the GMSC delegates the impression that the process of reconsideration would not take very long. But weeks went by, and so did a Conference of Local Medical Committees which was supposed to consider the Ministry's reply,[4] while the Ministry said nothing at all. Nothing is known officially about what happened during these weeks, but it seems certain that the Ministry's officials could not have spent the whole time talking out the

[1] *Ibid.*, 1949, II, Supp. 100–1; and 1950, I, Supp. 213.
[2] *Ibid.*, 1949, II, Supp. 127.
[3] *Ibid.*, 1949, II, 750 and Supp. 147.
[4] Members of the Conference of Local Medical Committees were elected to consider the Ministry's position at the Conference scheduled for October 27th.

subject among themselves; at any rate, in cases where interdepartmental negotiations have clearly not been involved, the Ministry has invariably been more prompt to formulate its case. The period in question, moreover, is that during which departments normally prepare the estimates for the financial year to come. Here again, therefore, questions of broader financial policy and interdepartmental relations appear to have affected decisively the course of the negotiations.

What bothered the Ministry at this time was not just the need to prepare a new set of estimates; that alone might, in fact, have made the Ministry more anxious to reach an amicable settlement with the profession, so that it could adjust in good time its financial plans. Rather, the really crucial difficulty arose from the failure of the Ministry once again to have estimated accurately the current year's expenditures. In February of 1950 it had to ask for yet another supplementary appropriation of £90 million, nearly 40 per cent of the estimate for 1949–50, once again for both good and bad reasons, which we need not go into here. But already in the autumn of 1949 officials at the Ministry must have known about the need for a second sizeable supplementary estimate and been in touch with the Treasury about it. We may presume that the furore which arose in public upon the actual introduction of the supplementary estimate was matched by a similar fuss in Whitehall in the autumn of 1949. Bevan must have been under considerable stress at that time, and his colleagues at the Treasury and in the Cabinet furious about the storm to come. Cripps in particular, having long been Bevan's champion, must have been very angry. Under these circumstances, Bevan and his officials could hardly have had much leeway for concessions, even concessions which might be anticipated in the coming set of estimates, for by that time the public issue was bound to be not accurate forecasting but the absolute cost of the Health Service, whether correctly predicted or not. That this was, in fact, the aspect of the problem which most bothered the Treasury was confirmed early in 1950 when Cripps, the Chancellor, set an absolute ceiling on the cost of the Service (£365 million for England and Wales). This, of course, was bound to make still more difficult the negotiations between the Ministry and the GMSC. From this point on all the negotiations proceeded under two stifling restraints: merciless public criticisms of the supplementary estimates and an intractable Treasury, absolutely determined to keep the cost of the Health Service within a limit predetermined by itself.

These facts should be kept in mind as background for the negotiations of 1950–51. For the moment, however, let us return to November 14, 1949, when Bevan at last replied to the GMSC's criticism of the Ministry's report of August. Bevan's reply, significantly, was made not in an informal meeting but through the medium of a formal letter: a step not calculated to produce a meeting of minds and used relatively rarely in negotiations about matters other than remuneration. The letter summarily rejected the GMSC's case. It conceded that larger allowances should have been made for increases in doctors and population, but argued that these were, in effect, taken care of by the opportunities of general practitioners to earn money additional to central pool funds (e.g. for maternity services, work in cottage hospitals, etc.); in any case, the *general economic situation* would not permit any increase, and no useful purpose would be served by further discussions.[1]

It took the GMSC officials two weeks to digest the Minister's letter and prepare a counter-plan. On December 1st a special meeting of the whole Committee was called at which Dr Frank Gray, next to Dr S. Wand the GMSC's most powerful figure, presented the leaders' views. The GMSC now was quite understandably in the mood to haggle. Having once demanded a £15.5 million increase in total remuneration,[2] it now made some curious statistical recalculations of its own and decided that a £7 million increase would be fair enough. This increase, it argued, could not be considered a raise in pay but an adjustment in the original settlement of terms of service, which, the BMA now realized, had been talked out insufficiently. A very high-powered delegation was appointed to go to the Ministry to press this case, a delegation tantamount to the BMA's informal 'cabinet'.[3] The delegation was received at the Ministry, but it accomplished nothing. Much correspondence followed, but still nothing could budge the Ministry's officials. They continued to talk about the limitations imposed by the general economic situation and absolutely refused to commit themselves on what were now the main issues: not whether adequate allowance had been made for increases in the number of doctors and population, but whether the Spens Report had been correctly translated into contemporary values in the first place and whether in the future the pool would be constantly adjusted in light of changes in values. In mid-March, finally, the GMSC's deputies gave up the struggle with the officials and asked to see the Minister himself. But by that date the time for concessions had surely passed. The estimates for 1950–51 were introduced on March 15th[4] and the decision to impose an inflexible ceiling on the cost of the Service had already been taken.

[1] *Ibid.*, 1949, II, Supp. 217.
[2] To bring the total up to the figure stated on page 134, make allowances for earnings outside the central pool.
[3] The Delegation included Drs S. Wand (the chairman of the GMSC), H. Guy Dain (a former chairman of the Council), E. A. Gregg (then Chairman of the Council), Frank Gray, W. Jope (Chairman of the Conference of LMCs) and W. M. Knox (the leader of the Scottish general practitioners).
[4] 472 *H. C. Deb.* 1087–91.

Still, Bevan, using his politician's skill to remarkable effect, did manage to soothe the GMSC. A meeting was arranged for April 13th, and Bevan, unlike his more cautious officials, did make some proposals which the GMSC's representatives received with reassurance. He would not promise to reconsider the Spens calculations, or any automatic adjustments in pay, but he would make large-scale inquiries into the actual incomes of doctors and the level of practice expenses under the Service, thus in effect re-opening the whole case while obviously playing for more time. The Committee, in turn, made some token concessions of its own, perhaps just to keep the negotiations alive; most important, it agreed to consider, if pressed to do so, some basis other than the faithful revaluation of the Spens proposals for calculating the size of the central pool.[1] The whole meeting was extremely cordial, the Bevan charm having its usual effect. Bevan graciously conceded the platitudes which the GMSC negotiators most liked to hear: that general practice could not be allowed to become the Cinderella of the Service and that general practitioners' incomes compared unfavourably with those of other members of the Service. He (Bevan) was 'not unsympathetic' to the doctors' case, but, after all, a general wage freeze was in effect, and Cripps had said that there could be no overall increase in the Health Service budget. If any part of the Service were given a larger appropriation, corresponding savings would have to be found elsewhere. In view of this, would the GMSC's delegation, asked Bevan, help him to find reasonable and prudent economies in the Service?[2] The delegates said they would and returned to BMA House, apparently in good spirits.

The Minister had promised to make the results of his inquiries available sometime in November; in the meantime matters were to rest. But the Bevan charm had clearly worn off by mid-June. The BMA's leaders were shocked by a letter from the Permanent Secretary of the Ministry, outlining the resolutions supposedly agreed to during the meeting with Bevan: the Ministry held that the profession had agreed to let the Minister introduce a new basis for calculating the central pool 'after the usual consultations'; the BMA's leaders insisted that they should not only be consulted but that their 'consent' should be required to make any such change. They wanted no unilateral decision-making by the Ministry, and because of this they now began to raise again an old question, sure to stir up trouble—the demand for compulsory arbitration.[3]

In fact, an even more ominous note now crept into their statements.

[1] *Ibid.*, 1950, I, Supp. 129.
[2] *Ibid.*, 1950, I, 997 and Supp. 168.
[3] *Ibid.*, 1950, I, Supp. 232 and 285.

In the event of disagreement and a refusal by the Ministry to arbitrate the dispute, the GMSC sought formal authority from the Conference of Local Medical Committees to prepare a mass withdrawal from the Service. This was given at the Conference of July 29th. The GMSC's leaders now refused to allow the Ministry to waste more time in undertaking inquiries and demanded an immediate resumption of discussions on the implementation of the Spens proposals and the question of arbitration. From now on, the threat of a mass withdrawal from the Service, however remote, hung over the negotiations.

The Negotiations, 1950–51

Late in July of 1950 the GMSC appointed another delegation to reformulate its case in consultation with its actuarial consultant. Shortly thereafter the delegates went to see the Ministry officials. We do not know exactly when the meeting took place or what was decided, but the GMSC's report of September 2nd states that sufficient agreement had been reached to allow factual inquiries to proceed.[1] Another oscillation in the Ministry's attitude clearly had taken place—once again at a time when estimates were not being prepared. At the same time, however, the British Medical Guild was asked to prepare for a mass withdrawal from the Service in case of an eventual deadlock. The Guild sent undated letters of resignation to general practitioners, asking that the letters be signed and returned, so that the Guild might produce them on a moment's notice in case negotiations again broke down,[2] a step hardly calculated to appease the Ministry. The profession's response, however, must have been heartening to the Government; at any rate, it explains why the threat of withdrawal did not get quick results. The GMSC's decision quickly revealed all the latent indiscipline and divisions in the profession. Individual practitioners proved on the whole to be extremely wary of signing blank resignations to be used at the leaders' discretion. Many were highly suspicious of the whole idea of the Medical Guild. When the GMSC announced that a 'strike' against the Service would have to be accompanied by a refusal to sign certificates (e.g. certificates required under the National Insurance Act) still more doctors openly expressed their reluctance to follow unconditionally the commands of their spokesmen. The Medical Practitioners Union, an organization of some 4,000 doctors, frequently at odds with the BMA, demanded a voice in the negotiations and signs of restiveness appeared among the specialists at the tough line taken by the GMSC.[3] As a result, the

[1] Ibid., 1950, II, Supp. 100.

[2] Ibid., 50, II, Supp. 135.

[3] The BMA's own Central Consultants and Specialists Committee, however, seems to have been in agreement with the GMSC. See British Medical Journal, 1951, Supp. 109.

Ministry won much valuable time while the BMA leaders tried to 'educate' the rank and file in the virtue of the Guild, the desirability of a strike against the Service, and the advisability of withholding certificates. The leaders still pretended to chafe under the Ministry's delays to publish factual information and make definite concessions; now they generously conceded, however, that the fault was not the Ministry's alone but due to certain circumstances beyond its control: disputes between doctors and tax inspectors over accounts to be used in determining contemporary practice expenses, delays in getting forms to the Executive Councils, etc.[1] The leaders were now only too willing to put off further action until late March of 1951, in the hope of overcoming the apathy of most members, and the actual opposition of many, before the meeting of a special conference scheduled for that time.

Three events of importance occurred, in addition to the strike threat, between the meeting of July 1950 and March 1951. First, Hugh Gaitskell replaced Sir Stafford Cripps as Chancellor of the Exchequer; through this step, Bevan lost one of his chief champions in the Cabinet, whatever the difficulties which had lately existed between Cripps and himself. Secondly, Bevan left the Ministry of Health (perhaps as the first step in his drift into opposition after the Korean period rearmament programme had been agreed upon) and was replaced by Hilary Marquand. Finally, a special committee, under the chairmanship of Sir Henry Cohen, was organized under the Central Health Services Council (the Minister's statutory professional advisory body on matters pertaining to the National Health Service) to study the conditions of general practice under the Service, including work loads, standards of practice, *and methods of remuneration.*

The organization of the Cohen Committee threw BMA House into consternation and one can easily understand why. In the first place, the Minister was threatening to bypass the GMSC altogether on the question of remuneration; the GMSC would be called upon to give evidence before the Cohen Committee but not to negotiate with it. In the second place, the Cohen Committee's own recommendations would not be binding on the Minister; indeed, the Minister had statutory power to suppress these recommendations altogether. In the third place, the membership of the Committee was uncongenial to the BMA. The Minister had not consulted it; and while the Committee included the Chairmen of the BMA Council, the Representative Body and the General Practice Review Committee,[2] most of its members (13 of 23) had had no recent experience with general practice and were believed to be unsympathetic to the BMA's case; a nasty leader in the *British*

---

[1] *Ibid.*, 1950, II, Supp. 182, 206, 221, and 259; and 1951, I, Supp. 21.
[2] Not to be confused with the GMSC.

Medical Journal called them 'a closed circus of trained performers'.[1] Sir Henry Cohen assured the BMA that his committee would only go into methods, not the level, of remuneration,[2] but the GMSC was not reassured, perhaps because the method largely determines the level. In a significant letter to the Local Medical Committees it asked the latter 'not to offer or agree to give evidence direct to the general practice committee of the CHSC' but to let the GMSC 'co-ordinate the views of the local medical committees in order to embody them in evidence in due course'[3]—a request which speaks for itself. The organization of the Cohen Committee did more than stir up misgivings in the BMA: it restored the sense of urgency which the mixed reception of the GMSC's threat to withdraw from the Service had dispelled. On pains of being bypassed altogether, the BMA leaders now could not afford to let negotiations await the re-education of the members.

The Cohen Committee was organized at the beginning of February 1951; on February 22nd negotiations between officials of the Ministry and delegates of the GMSC were resumed. The subject was relatively innocuous: the proportion of gross income to be deducted for practice expenses to arrive at the net incomes of general practitioners. The two parties were remarkably close in the percentages they suggested: the Association's actuary suggested 37·5 per cent, the Ministry's actuary 36·5 per cent. Yet so strained had relations become since the 'strike' threat had been raised on one side and the threat to bypass the BMA on the other, that the negotiators could not agree on a mean of 37 per cent. The Association, indeed, went so far as to ask for a special meeting with Marquand on the issue and organized a very high-powered delegation to see him (this was, after all, to be their first official meeting); in the meantime, private talks were also held between an important member of the Secretariat and the Permanent Secretary of the Ministry.[4] Clearly the issue ostensibly at stake did not call for contacts at so high a level. Their purpose surely was to make fruitful discussions at lower levels possible by re-establishing good relations at the top, an inference confirmed by the fact that the GMSC asked the Minister to discuss also at the proposed meeting the competence of the Cohen Committee and 'general principles' to govern a settlement.[5]

Marquand immediately met the GMSC representatives (February

---

[1] *British Medical Journal*, 1951, I, 342 and Supp. 34.
[2] *Ibid.*, 1951, I, Supp. 45.
[3] *Ibid.*, 1951, I, Supp. 49.
[4] *Ibid.*, 1951, I, Supp. 61. The delegation included Drs Wand, Jope, Gregg, Dain, Davies, Gray, and Knox (see note 3, p. 139), plus Dr Sutherland (the chairman of the BMA's important Amending Acts Committee) and the Association's actuary.
[5] *British Medical Journal*, loc. cit.

28th) and assumed a very friendly and understanding attitude. He conceded that there was a good *prima facie* case for reviewing, as a matter of urgency, the adequacy of total remuneration of general practitioners and its distribution, and he asked for a further meeting before the end of April; in the meantime he would acquaint himself more thoroughly with the situation. He made some ominous comments about current economic problems and the large cost of rearmament, but the whole atmosphere of the meeting was cordial, as was the atmosphere of the Conference of Local Medical Committees held a month later.[1] Dr Wand, speaking for the GMSC, praised Marquand's co-operative attitude, asked indulgence for him because he was 'new to the job,' dangled before the conference the inviting prospect of a change in the Permanent Secretaryship in the Ministry, mentioned the proximity of budget day, and counselled caution and delay with regard to the mass resignations.[2] Three motions by Local Medical Committees counselling a speedy boycott of the Service should the Minister not grant the whole of the GMSC's case were overwhelmingly defeated.[3] Another oscillation, this time on both sides.

There matters rested until early May, when Dr Wand obtained a private interview with Marquand, during which arrangements were made to have the Minister receive a full deputation from the GMSC on May 9th. A very long meeting (six hours) took place on that date.[4] Its outcome, and that of a subsequent exchange by correspondence—itself an indication of a breakdown of good relations—were just what might have been expected. Alas, said the Minister, the budget had put a hard and fast ceiling on the cost of the Health Service; the Ministry therefore could not add more than two million to the central pool, however just in the abstract the profession's claims might be; this increase could itself be granted only on certain conditions: that a corresponding saving could be made in the drug bill, that the maximum numbers of patients on practitioners' lists would be reduced below the level of 4,000 and that the additional money would be applied wholly to make it easier for new doctors to enter general practice and to improve the position of those with small lists (presumably by 'weighting' patients).[5] In short: no increase anywhere in the Service that could not be matched by savings elsewhere in the Service, and nothing more for general practitioners

---

[1] *Ibid.*, 1951, I, 515 and Supp. 81.

[2] *Ibid.*, 1951, I, Supp. 141.

[3] However, a motion was carried to widen the scope of the conditions under which withdrawal from the Service would take place, to include a refusal by the Ministry to arbitrate an irreconcilable disagreement. The purpose of this motion, quite explicitly, was to obtain stronger support for a future boycott by mobilizing professional opposition on a popular issue.

[4] *British Medical Journal*, 1951, I, Supp. 241.

[5] Letter from the Ministry, dated May 23, 1951. See also *British Medical Journal*, 1951, I, Supp. 241 ff.

without a change in distribution methods which now favoured the most powerful element in the BMA, well-established general practitioners. To achieve such a change in distribution, the Minister proposed that a Working Party be organized to explore details; and to obtain the additional funds the Minister suggested that the profession curtail all excessive prescribing. Marquand was particularly anxious to obtain agreement with the BMA on distribution methods which would give a greater chance to unestablished doctors to establish themselves independently in practice, rather than having to work hard on scanty salaries as assistants to established doctors. He considered the difficulties young general practitioners had in entering the service as principals to be one of its most unmitigated evils, and resented the hypocrisy of established doctors who, while verbally opposed to all forms of salaried service, 'ran a sort of salaried service for younger doctors themselves'.[1]

We can imagine the fury these proposals generated in the BMA when we note that in its response the Association raised again, for no very apparent reason, all the bogeys about remuneration forgotten since August of 1948. The Ministry's proposals, argued a leader in the *Journal*, would bring closer a whole-time salaried service [*sic*] and make more difficult the free choice of doctor by patients; the 'casual bait' of £2 million was designed to divert the profession from its sacred insistence on Spens and nothing less than Spens; it was the thin end of the wedge, to be followed by still greater and swifter departures from the Spens formula.[2] The GMSC, for its part, accused Marquand of breach of promise and sanctimoniously pointed out that the doctor's first duty was to his patients, who should not be deprived of medication so that practitioners might have a reasonable income; it therefore refused to join any working party on the terms proposed by the Minister and proposed to consider joining such a party only if it could review the whole condition of general practice.

At this point, however, the Minister was clearly unwilling to risk an absolute and final rift. In a letter written a week after his initial proposals he agreed to let the proposed Working Party discuss a wider range of issues, provided they would lead to changes in distribution along the lines he had suggested. He also promised that the Cohen Committee would normally consult the GMSC before reaching any decisions. The GMSC pounced upon these olive branches and used them for all they were worth. It insisted, as a matter of principle, that the central pool should be determined not by budgetary expediency but along the lines of Spens; it pointed out that by this time the cost of living had gone up further, making necessary a betterment factor of around 100 per cent

---

[1] Letter to the author from the Rt. Hon. Hilary A. Marquand, March, 2 1959.
[2] *British Medical Journal*, 1951, I, 1372.

instead of 70 per cent; that practice expenses had risen too, from 37·5 per cent to at least 40 per cent, that the number of doctors had increased, and so also their volume of work. All this made the Minister's offer of £2 million even more ludicrous than it had appeared at first. It was clear to the GMSC that matters had come to a final deadlock. Under the circumstances, it revived a proposal now dormant for a considerable period—arbitration. Let the proper size of the central pool be determined by an impartial referee; then the profession would consider how best to distribute the pool 'in accordance with the Spens Committee' and so as to 'enable the best possible medical services to be available to the public'.[1] A Special Conference of Local Medical Committees held on July 19th endorsed this proposal, after Dr Wand of the GMSC had made a rather bellicose speech, charging the Ministry with trying to split the profession by playing against one another the interests of specialists and general practitioners, by making increases in general practitioners' remuneration dependent on decreases elsewhere in the Service. The spectre of the salaried service—a very remote danger, considering that the Minister envisaged little more than weighting patients by 'loadings payments'—was again conjured up; and the Spens proposals were again endorsed as criteria beyond compromise.[2]

It was now clear to everyone that the negotiations had failed, and that the *force* available to one side or the other would determine the outcome, if there was to be no arbitration. But what force was available to either side? It was doubtful that the BMA could organize an effective mass withdrawal from the Health Service, or that the Ministry could prevent all breakdowns in the Service, once the Medical Guild was called into action. It was doubtful that the GMSC could now justify to the doctors any settlement short of Spens, or that the Ministry could capitulate by granting a settlement fully up to Spens. There was only one way out, and Marquand took it. Early in August he agreed to withdraw his previous proposals and, for all practical purposes, to accept arbitration. An independent investigator, acceptable to both parties, should be appointed to determine the proper size of the pool under Spens, having proper regard to other sources of income of general practitioners and to the changes in income in other professions. Simultaneously, a working party of the GMSC and the Ministry should be constituted to work out a new distribution scheme to discourage large lists and make it easier for doctors to establish themselves in practice. Marquand declared himself prepared to accept the adjudicator's findings, subject to the overriding authority of Parliament and subject to an agreement on distribution

[1] *Ibid.*, 1951, I, Supp. 263.
[2] *Ibid.*, 1951, II, Supp. 29.

being reached.[1] For its part, the GMSC also agreed, provided only that the working party were given broader authority to settle all questions of distribution based on Spens, and that the adjudicator be given precise terms of reference on which to base a decision (by implication also the Spens proposals).[2]

A newly constituted delegation of powerful GMSC members[3] met Ministry officials (subsequently also the Minister) late in September to discuss procedures for arbitration. Agreement was quickly reached. Terms of reference to govern the working party were agreed to as follows:

'To secure an equitable distribution of the Central Pool based upon the recommendations of the Spens Committee, the object being to enable the best possible medical service to be available to the public, and to safeguard the standard of medical service by discouraging unduly large lists: at the same time, to bring about a relative improvement in the position of those practitioners least favourably placed under the present plan of distribution; to make it easier for new doctors to enter service, and to stimulate group practice.'

Terms of reference to govern the adjudicator (who was to be a High Court judge) were stated thus:

'To determine the size of the Central Pool after taking account of remuneration from all other sources received by general practitioners, in order to give effect to the recommendations of the Spens Committee, having regard to the change in the value of money since 1939, to the increases which have taken place in incomes in other professions, and to all other relevant factors.'

Finally, while both sides agreed that the working party should function as a team the Ministry did not rule out the possibility of arbitration in event of disagreement.[4]

The BMA, with good reason, was well pleased with this arrangement. At the Annual Conference of Representatives of Local Medical Committees, Dr Wand reviewed the negotiations leading to the arbitration agreement. The talks had gone on for a long time, he said. In some instances it had been a case of the survival of the fittest. 'I think', he said, 'we have survived.'[5]

The Outcome and Its Significance

In December, Mr Justice Danckwerts of the High Court of Justice

---

[1] Ibid., 1951, II, Supp. 56.
[2] Ibid., 1951, II, Supp. 69.
[3] With a membership almost identical with those of previous delegations, (including Drs Wand, Campbell, Dain, Davies, Gray, Knox, and Rogers).
[4] Ibid., 1951, II, Supp. 153.
[5] Ibid., 1951, II, Supp. 197.

was invited by the Lord Chancellor to act as adjudicator, and here we may end the story. When the question of the determination of the central pool passed to 'adjudication' it ceased to be a matter for Ministry–BMA relations, so that there is no point here in reviewing the representations made to Justice Danckwerts. We might briefly state, however, for their interest, the decisions reached by Justice Danckwerts and the Working Party, and analyse the principal lessons of the protracted negotiations.

The decision of Justice Danckwerts, handed down on March 24, 1952, completely vindicated the BMA's interpretation of the Spens proposals. Danckwerts applied a betterment factor of 100 per cent for 1952 and of 85 per cent for 1948, and used a percentage of 38·7 per cent for practice expenses, both higher than the BMA's original claims. For the year immediately past, this meant an addition of nearly 10 million pounds to the central pool, and, since the award was made retroactive to the beginning of the Service, a total award of about 40 million pounds to general practitioners. The real victory of the BMA, however, came not in the determination of these generous figures but in the Ministry's concession, when it agreed to arbitration, that the Spens proposals rather than current economic policy should determine the remuneration of general practitioners in the Service. The Joint Working Party of the Ministry and the BMA, on the other hand, agreed to the changes in the scheme of distribution desired by the Ministry. Maximum lists were reduced from 4,000 to 3,500 patients (but on the understanding that the incomes of doctors whose lists were reduced would still be slightly increased); a special 'loadings payment' of 10 shillings per patient would be paid for patients in the range 501 to 1,500 on doctors' lists; the 'basic salary' was abolished and replaced by an 'initial practice allowance' of 600 pounds, 450 pounds, and 200 pounds, payable only in the first, second and third years of practice, i.e. while new practitioners built up their lists. Both parties quickly agreed to these decisions.[1]

Who won? Clearly the BMA had the better of the argument in the end. Not only did it obtain the increase in pay it had demanded for three years—indeed, slightly more than it had demanded—but it had forced the Government to adhere to the Spens proposal, it had obtained arbitra-on, and it had gained the abolition of the much disliked basic salary. Nevertheless, the final settlement had some of the characteristics of a *quid pro quo*. There was little enthusiasm in the BMA for the new distribution scheme, and the initial practice allowance was little more than the basic salary under an alias, more restricted on paper, but in some cases actually easier to grant to unestablished doctors.[2] The distribution

[1] A summary of the decisions may be found in Ross, *National Health Service in Great Britain*, pp. 387–89.
[2] There were some differences, of course, between the old basic salary and

of spoils corresponded roughly, in my opinion, to the merits of the positions taken by the two sides. So far as the size and determination of the central pool was concerned, the BMA had an unassailable moral case: general practitioners had entered the Service with the understanding that the Spens proposals would be implemented fairly and that the disagreements about them would be proper subjects for arbitration. The presentation of its case certainly was badly timed at every turn, but that does not affect its merits. The Ministry, on the other hand, could only plead the general economic situation in defence, but it would be difficult to make a moral (not economic) case for inflicting on the nationalized doctors burdens which the unnationalized professions did not have to bear. On the other hand, the Service as such would have been improved little by an increase in pay that did not accrue chiefly to men with small lists, especially doctors starting new practices in under-doctored areas. So, in the end, the doctors got what they wanted, and the country got an improved general practitioner service.

Nevertheless, the negotiations were anything but an unqualified success. From the standpoint of BMA–Ministry relations they must indeed be considered a complete failure. The negotiations took a long time (more than two years of discussions on a problem which Justice Danckwerts settled in a week). They produced a good deal of bad feeling, though bad feeling mitigated somewhat by a mutual understanding of the forces that produced intransigence. At one point they even threatened, remotely to be sure, a breakdown of the Service. And, not least, they led to a vindication of a method for calculating general practitioner remuneration—faithful adherence to the vague, problem-charged recommendations of the Spens Committee—which promised only similar difficulties in the future, and has been responsible for more bad feeling and bad reasoning than any other aspect of the Service.

In the final analysis, the negotiations failed simply because they could only lead to a decision to abandon them. They could produce no result until tranferred to other hands; and they had to be abandoned not only because the Spens criteria turned out to be nearly as bad as no criteria at all, but because neither side had the force or the freedom of manoeuvre required to achieve a settlement within the boundaries of negotiation. In the case of the Ministry, the stumbling block clearly was the Treasury. If we cast our minds back over the detailed course of the negotiations, we find that, at first, its role as the *eminence grise* of the

---

the new Initial Practice Allowance. The IPA can be given for only three years, while the old basic salary could (but generally did not) go on for years, tapering off as the doctor's list increased. The IPA is also paid automatically in 'designated' (that is, badly under-doctored) areas, while the basic salary could be paid to any new practitioner who could make out a case for it.

K*

negotiations is almost imperceptible; but as the discussions proceed we see the Ministry wavering more and more between cordiality and hostility, hostility always following long gaps in the discussions during which interdepartmental discussion must have taken place and coming at times when the estimates are in preparation; more significant still, as the negotiations proceed, the refusal by the Ministry of GMSC proposals is couched more and more in terms of the general economic situation and justified explicitly by invoking Treasury decisions; in the end, the impasse is made final by the Treasury's decision to put an absolute limit on National Health Service expenditures. The Ministry was in an impossible position: it could not override the Chancellor, but it had to run the Health Service, i.e. maintain good relations with the profession, a fact which explains its schizophrenic and exasperating wavering between sympathy and antipathy. The BMA, on the other hand, was under enormous pressure to achieve a sizeable increase in pay but quite unable, for all its tough gestures, to utilize its only effective weapon for unilaterally compelling an increase: a large-scale strike against the Service. Its rank and file was far too apathetic, too hostile to trade union tactics and too much afflicted by internal divisions—divisions emphasized by the acute anxiety of the GMSC that local Medical Committees might independently give evidence before the Cohen Committee.

We have every reason to think that these factors would produce similar tensions and crises in other negotiations about general practitioner remuneration—in fact, they have, and with a vengeance. But the sequel to the negotiations over Spens of 1948–52—the even more acrimonious negotiations of 1955–56 which, had it not been for the intervention of the specialists, might actually have come to an attempted mass withdrawal from the Service—lie outside our scope and tell us nothing we do not know already.

VII

Postscript

THE SIGNIFICANCE OF
PRESSURE GROUP POLITICS

The activities of any pressure group or set of pressure groups constitute what the sociologists call a 'system': an ordered pattern of relations. These activities take place within larger systems (the political system, the social system) which impinge upon them and upon which they impinge. There are consequently, speaking very broadly, two ways in which one can theorize about pressure groups, or any other social activities. One can focus inquiry on the sub-system, the pressure group, raising questions about its nature and the factors that affect it, including among these factors the larger system in which it operates. Or one can focus inquiry on the larger system, raising questions about the significance within it of any pattern of pressure group activity which it comprehends.

Throughout this study my theoretical concerns have been with the sub-system: with the determinants of the form of any pattern of pressure group politics, of its scope and intensity, and its effectiveness; broader aspects of the political and social system and of 'culture' (patterns of beliefs and values) have been touched upon only in so far as they help one to answer these questions. But pressure group analyses have long been concerned also with theorizing of the second sort. Indeed, the study of pressure groups began largely with such theorizing. The muckrakers in America were interested in pressure groups as sinister influences which tend to undermine democratic processes; hence, they did not raise questions about the manner in which larger social institutions affect pressure groups, but were concerned almost entirely with the impingement of pressure groups on what they conceived to be the proper functioning of larger social units, specifically of democratic systems. Out of their disillusion with the operation of formal democratic processes emerged the 'scientific' school of pressure group analysis: theorists who, while preserving—sometimes with thinly disguised difficulty—an attitude of normative neutrality toward pressure groups, maintained that the operation of political systems could be fully described in terms of the conflict of groups within it; that the formal institutions did not matter, or mattered only in that as they themselves represented group interests. Bentley, the undoubted founder of this very influential school, stated nothing less than that all social relations—'the whole social life in all its phases'—could be stated in terms of groups of active men. 'When the groups are adequately stated', he expostulated, 'everything is stated. When I say everything I mean everything.' Modern apostles of this gospel have not made many concessions to attract those of us who remain largely unconverted; nearly fifty years after Bentley the group approach still stands as one of the chief approaches to political science and claims of Bentleyan flamboyance are still made for it.[1]

Emerging from these two strands of thought, two questions have dominated theorizing about the significance of pressure group politics within the larger political system. First, how far can the analysis of group pressures and conflicts of pressures take us in describing and explaining political systems as such? Second, do pressure groups tend to support or corrode democratic systems? To these one should add perhaps a third question which has emerged from the much more modern use by political scientists of 'functional' theories, a question which both adds to and comprehends the other two. What contributions do pressure groups make to the political system as a whole, and do these contributions tend to make the system more or less viable (stable, effective)? Are their consequences 'dysfunctional' or 'eufunctional' for the larger systems in which they operate?

These questions, as I have said, are not my principal theoretical concerns here. Moreover, one hesitates to comment on them in passing, for anyone can see that they are very difficult and not to be taken lightly. But they are of greater concern to many political scientists than the more modest questions on which I have concentrated; and the case-study does, I think, shed some light on them, as indeed—if the questions are sensible questions to begin with—it must. I shall conclude, therefore, with some comments on them.

The Group Approach
When we have stated the groups involved in British medical politics

[1] Note the following: '. . . political science has as its chief problem the authoritative allocation of values and . . . the means by which those values are allocated is the group struggle.' What of individuals? 'The individual has many facets and these are reflections of the groups in which he is a participant.' What of formal institutions? 'An institution is a stable group of individual activities.' And ideas, values? 'Ideas are expressions in verbal or other forms of activity, and in the governmental process they also take their meaning from the group association.' See Charles B. Hagan, 'The Group in a Political Science', *Approaches to The Study of Politics* (ed. Young), *passim*.

have we stated everything there is to state about the subject? We can,
of course, use the concept 'group' in such a way that it becomes impossible to answer no, and most of the more audacious group theorists do
precisely that when asked to account for any specific policy. Of course,
they admit that governmental institutions do not simply ring up the
outcome of group conflicts like mere cash registers but themselves make
or help to make decisions; but governmental institutions may be
represented as groups and participants in the group struggle (as 'official
groups', for example)[1] and so the theory stands. Sometimes clear-cut
majority mandates are given and, for all intents and purposes, close an
issue; but then the group theorist simply adds the 'majority group' to his
universe, and so again the theory stands. Sometimes, conditions in a
society are such that policy is adopted which is not promoted by any
pressure groups; but then the theory is saved by distinguishing manifest
and latent interests and manifest and latent interest groups. Sometimes
an individual—a Bevan, a Guy Dain—seems to play a decisive role; but
that does not stump the group theorists either, for what are individuals
if not agglutinated heaps of group identifications?

So interpreted, the group approach undoubtedly tells us all there is
to know about British medical politics or any other kind of politics, but
only by allowing us to state in group language what otherwise we would
state in different terms. As used by its more extravagant exponents,
group theory tends indeed to become nothing more than a language,
based on the plausible but arbitrary metaphysic that in politics the
ultimately 'real', the component alike of individuals and institutions,
the unit which really 'acts' and underlies ideas, is the group—not
individuals, interactions, institutions, or larger political systems.
Nothing can escape the clutches of this metaphysics if only one stretches
it far enough, but precisely because of this nothing is illuminated by it
either.

If we state group theory in a starker and less comprehensive form we
can make debatable, and therefore illuminating, assertions in terms of it.
We could assert, for example, that the cash register theory of political
group conflict does indeed hold always, or a good deal of the time, in
democratic systems: that policy is generally a sort of necessary, even
mathematical, product of the objective power and intensity of interest
of the private groups which exert pressure upon the policy-makers. Then
some very interesting questions would arise. Under what conditions, and
how generally, do public decision-making bodies in fact act like machines
that register group pressures? What, if any, is the role of mandates
given by the electorate compared to such pressures? What influence is
exerted upon the content of policy by the form of the decision-making

[1] See Earl Latham, *The Group Basis of Politics*, Cornell U. P., 1952, pp. 33–53.

structure that formulates it, independently of group pressure? How do broadly shared attitudes mitigate group conflict? How does the pressure of the 'setting', of given conditions, modify the pressure of groups? Can individual decision-makers ever really transcend the environment of pressure brought to bear upon them? Are they more able to do so in some systems than in others?

The moment we deal with mandates, formal institutions, and cultural attitudes in group terms, these questions seem to evaporate; but they are always precipitated upon us again in a slightly different form. We may assert that anything may be stated in terms of groups; but then we tend merely to restate our questions rather than to answer them. Instead of inquiring into the role of the 'electorate', we then inquire into the role of 'majority interest groups'; instead of inquiring into the role of formal institutions, we then inquire into the role of the institutionalized myths of the dominant groups. Is there really a difference between one and the other? Shifting group pressures may, to be sure, help explain changes in formal institutions and in political culture themselves; but until it is demonstrated that these and other factors relevant to political decision-making have no autonomy at all—that they always play dependent variable to the independent variables of the group conflict—we surely gain nothing by stating them as if they were group phenomena, except perhaps a greater imprecision of language. What is the use of trying to state everything as statements about groups, if that forces us to make new distinctions where older distinctions, and distinctions easier to grasp, already exist?

For these reasons, in asking here whether British medical politics can be 'stated' fully in terms of the groups concerned in it, I mean the question to be taken in the starkest and narrowest possible sense: is medical policy really made by the BMA, limited only by the competition it evokes among other private groups? This question is not so uncompromisingly phrased as to make a negative answer to it a foregone conclusion. The answer to it in fact is, yes—at any rate to a great extent. In saying that British medical policy has simply been BMA policy, we leave out surprisingly little from the account we must give of actual British medical policy. We do leave out some things. We leave out the pressure of events and of conditions; any account of the origins of the Health Service, for example, must take into consideration the awful faults of the pre-Health Service system and the role of the war in bringing these faults to public attention, as I have tried to show elsewhere.[1] We leave out generally shared social values, and their expression through party policy and electoral mandates; the National Health Service, again, cannot be fully explained without reference to the

[1] See Eckstein, *The English Health Service*, Chapters 3 and 4.

collectivist streak ingrained in British political attitudes,[1] its crystallization in party programmes during the war, the large mandate given the Labour Party in 1945, and the insulation against group pressure this gave the Ministry, at least for a time. Nor can we omit such broadly shared attitudes from an account of BMA attitudes themselves, although that is another matter. We leave out, to a less important extent, the intrinsic requirements of having to administer a statutory policy—less important because, in the one case this has played a role, the Registrar disputes, it did not play a narrowly constricting role. We leave out the role of the Treasury, which illustrates not only the autonomous role of formal institutions in policy-making but also the role of environmental conditions, in this case the economic problems of Britain in the post-war period.

This series of omitted factors may sound imposing, and from the standpoint of general theory it is. But the fact remains that, in a purely quantitative sense, we need not invoke these factors to account for very much, provided only that we equate BMA attitudes with the viewpoints actually pressed at the level of government. This, however, tells us nothing about the general validity of the group approach to politics, as I have stated it. It only tells us that there is a good deal in it under certain conditions. What then are the conditions which maximize the influence of groups ?

This question, it might be noted before we attempt to answer it, is not the same as that raised in Chapter I about the effectiveness of pressure groups. There we were concerned with the effectiveness of pressure groups in relation to other pressure groups as well as other elements involved in policy-making; here we are concerned with the influence of groups relative only to the other elements: the significance of group competition as well as the significance of single groups in the decision-making process. But while these are different questions, the answers to them need not be very different; and where groups confront relatively little opposition from other groups, where the chief competition is between a group on one hand and parties, formal institutions and broad public opinion on the other, the answers will inevitably tend to be the same.

In the simplest terms, group influence is enlarged by anything which restricts the influence on policy-making of anything else. This either is or comes close to being a tautology, but is none the less worth stating. For example, the influence of groups certainly is enhanced by the lack of any wide public interest in an area of policy, simply because such lack of interest, apart from minimizing group competition, tends to neutralize some of the more important centres of influence which compete with

[1] See Beer and Ulam, *Patterns of Government*, pp. 161–164.

private groups as such. Parties, to be sure, do sometimes propose policy merely for the sake of having a programme, but generally they concern themselves with issues which are of wide public concern. That goes also for the press, especially the popular press, and for Parliament. Here once again consensus is a matter of crucial importance, but not consensus alone. Public interest and the chief organs which express and arouse it may also be diverted from an area of policy by the feeling that the subject involved is not the public's business, e.g. by the conviction that it is a field only for the technically competent. We can see both considerations at work in the striking shift from near-impotence to near-omnipotence which occurred in the BMA's position between the passage of the National Health Service Act and the Appointed Day. There occurred in this period a corresponding shift from profound to much shallower public interest (at any rate, until the Appointed Day itself drew near) and from considerations of general policy to considerations of detail; in fact the very fact that Parliament drew up such a very skeletal piece of legislation in the Health Service Act denotes its willingness to abdicate its own influence (and the influence of Party) to that of technically specialized groups.

Similarly, group influence is enhanced by anything which restricts the interest of formal governmental institutions other than Parliament, especially the administrative departments. Interdepartmental interest is, of course, tepid where policies impinge relatively little on a variety of administrative concerns; with the exception of its financial aspects this has been so in the case of medical policy. It is also diminished by the factors which diminish broad public interest itself: by agreement and the recognition of technical incompetence. Finally, it is diminished, even where interdepartmental concerns are impinged upon, by the presence of a powerful Minister as spokesman for the policy concerned.

The group theory of politics emerges from this discussion as a powerful heuristic tool, but only for the analysis of certain kinds of political systems and certain kinds of policies within such systems. It is most useful of all wherever there exists a great amount of agreement on basic political issues and a high degree of concern with narrowly delimited policies impinging upon technical, especially professionalized, fields. This is hardly surprising, either in itself or in the light of the conditions (discussed in Chapter I[1]) under which private groups tend to become politically active as pressure groups. But it does help us to understand the enormous influence of pressure groups on British medical policy; and perhaps it helps us to understand also why the group approach to politics has been influential mainly in the Anglo-Saxon countries and scored its greatest triumphs in the age of the social welfare state.

[1] See above, p. 26 ff.

Pressure Groups and the Democratic Process

Much of what I have said about the group theory of politics is also relevant to an even older issue: whether pressure groups in democratic systems are a good or a bad thing, conducive or not to the 'national interest', aids or hindrances to the operation of democratic procedures. It has proved extraordinarily difficult to deal with these questions; and most positions taken on them in the past do more to beg them than to answer them. Nor do these questions answer themselves in light of what has been said here about the conditions under which intensive pressure group activity emerges. For something may very well be both a symptom of health and corrosive of health; such neat, uncomfortable contradictions do sometimes arise in nature no less than in Germanic ideologies. The position on the question suggested by this study, however, is much more reassuring. In a nutshell, the study suggests (to me, at any rate) that the influence of private groups is greatest when, from the standpoint of democratic values, it matters least whether it is great or small.

Those who abominate pressure groups as influences which distort democratic processes do so for very simple reasons. They believe that pressure group activity leads to the satisfaction of particular interests to the detriment of general interests. They also believe that it shifts the arena of decision-making from the public limelight to the 'backstairs', where collusion and manipulation become possible because normal democratic controls do not operate—collusion not only against the public at large but frequently also against the rank and file of the pressure groups themselves. 'Light! More light!' exclaims Professor Finer at the end of his otherwise dry and laconic study of the British 'lobby', while Mr Mackenzie, in concluding his ground breaking essay on British pressure groups, conjures up the awful prospect of a 'new medievalism', where a man 'is socially important only as the holder of standard qualifications and as a member of authorized groups'.[1] These writers do not argue that pressure groups have no uses at all, or that nothing can be done to make them more 'responsible'. They do imply that the uses of groups like the BMA are vitiated by the 'too-close embrace' of Ministry and Association: by the latter's ability to force its sectional interests, through all too confidential negotiations, upon the Government. Is this a legitimate criticism?

It is true that relations between the BMA and the Ministry are, more often than not, highly confidential, even secret; but is it really obvious that this is a bad thing? As in the conduct of foreign relations, something is certainly to be said for secrecy in this case, at least at certain stages of the negotiations. We know from experience that the exposure of negotia-

[1] W. J. M. Mackenzie, 'Pressure Groups in British Government,' *British Journal of Sociology*, June, 1955, p. 146.

tions to the public while they are in process is one way to make them fail; the Ministry tends to assume a pose calculated to avert awkward interventions by Parliament or other departments; the BMA's leaders act so as to appear to be stubbornly pushing the members' 'interests'; all the latent pressures and limiting factors which prevent free accommodation between Ministry and Association tend to become mobilized. Even where outside interventions do not actually occur they tend to be anticipated, the results being the same. If it is at all desirable that there should be exchanges between the Ministry and the Association aiming at agreement, then it is desirable that their transactions should be confidential—perhaps not always and at every stage, but surely to a large extent.

Anyhow, who would take much interest in these transactions? Negotiations nowadays tend to be confidential not so much because of any anti-democratic collusion among the negotiators, but, much more important, because very few people really care about them. Nor is that really a bad thing. It is the result of the same factors which maximize pressure group activity and pressure group influence: a high degree of consensus on fundamental policy and the shift of disputes (partly because of fundamental agreement, partly for other reasons) to technical issues which most people do not and need not understand. Whenever any fundamental, widely interesting matters have arisen between the Ministry and BMA—money matters, questions of good faith towards the doctors in the Service—the normal machinery of publicity we associate with democracy has in fact swung into action and negotiations have been well aired (to their detriment). In other cases, we are almost always told the broad course and outcome of negotiations, if not the more intimate details, and this regardless of the state of public interest; the difficulty is not so much that information is not available but that it is uninteresting, not of public concern, and therefore largely ignored by Parliament and the Press. This also is not symptomatic of any malaise in the machinery of democracy but a sign of health, for enterprises like the National Health Service would be notorious only if they were highly controversial—or very badly managed.

Of course, even when negotiations are widely publicized we rarely learn who is really 'responsible' for decisions. The originators of positions, the makers of compromises, the mediators and the recalcitrants remain anonymous. It is always the Minister who appears before the House and the Chairman who appears before the Council or the ARM to take responsibility, although we know that they enter personally into very few negotiations, and even then, generally speaking, only when they have broken down. The real work is done by the shadowy junta of Assistant Secretaries. But if that is bad, then the whole British parliamentary system is an abomination, for one of its basic suppositions is that it is enough that *someone* should be accountable for decisions, not that it must be the person actually responsible. Like secrecy, this doctrine also has great utility: it produces decisions rather than procrastinations; like secrecy, too, it never keeps real controversies from being really argued.

In this case at least, the empire of the lobby is anonymous, when it is and to the extent that it is anonymous, because of constitutional processes and public apathy; and so much the better. But is it constructive, in a broad national sense, in the decisions it produces? Does it promote general or sectional interests?

That decisions relating to medical policy are made in Britain by the interaction of 'authorized groups' is undeniable. In negotiations about such policy the general public plays no role, except only when its views are 'represented' by the Treasury. But that again is not very serious: what views, after all, are there to represent? More seriously, even medical views are stated only through the medium of the oligarchy, which is itself a kind of specially 'authorized' group *vis-à-vis* the Ministry and not ordinarily representative, in the strict sense, of the profession. But does that matter any more than the relatively free hand of the Ministry? The power of the oligarchy, as we have seen, rests to a large extent on apathy, and apathy in turn reflects not merely the individualistic habits of the profession but also the uncontroversial character of the oligarchy's attitudes. Whenever the leaders have been seriously out of tune with a large proportion of the members on seriously controversial issues, the members have generally managed to exert some independent weight. Only rarely, to be sure, have they been able actually to convert the leaders, who have generally continued to play an autonomous role in negotiations (e.g. in the earlier negotiations over the National Health Service); but, on the other hand, the dissidents have been able to give to the Ministry tactical advantages (playing off one section of the profession against another, for example) which have had important effects on negotiations. As in the case of secrecy, which is great only when public interest is slight, so also here the discretion of the oligarchs is greatest when it matters least. Of course, nothing like a direct flow of views from the rank and file ever takes place; but then it never does.

Perhaps one may more reasonably object to the virtual exclusion from medical negotiations of 'unauthorized' groups like the Medical Practitioners Union (which has two members on the GMSC, where they exert little influence) and the Socialist Medical Association. Neither, however, is very significant numerically, while still other medical corporations, like the Royal Colleges, do play a role when their interests are aroused, infrequently though that is the case.

However, the fact that medical policies are not made by collusion among a few specially privileged leaders—at any rate not more than is inevitable in the nature of the case—does not mean necessarily that the policies are always in the general interest. But how can one readily determine whether they are in the 'general interest' or not? If we could know objectively what the general interest is, no difficulty about this would arise; but I for one have no idea how to determine an objective general interest. Only three questions, it seems to me, allow one to deal with the problem with any precision at all. We can ask, first, whether the policies adopted seem to be what most people seem to want, taking the public interest to be any action broadly desired by the public. The answer in that case is simply that most people appear to have no strong preferences, if any preferences at all, on the sort of subjects negotiations between the BMA and Ministry have covered. There may be a 'latent' general interest in these negotiations, but on the level of manifest and broad social purposes medical negotiations have been virtually irrelevant. We can ask, second, whether public medical services would have been more effective—whatever that may mean: a lower death rate? less suffering? more cures for less money?—if the BMA had been less effective, less intimately involved in medical policy-making. The best answer to that probably is that without such intimate involvement there might be no public medical services at all; but, apart from that, how could one possibly tell what policy could have been under other conditions? Third, we can ask whether, due to BMA pressure, the medical services have been withdrawing too large a share from total national wealth, relative to other services: whether they have encroached unduly on the generalizable resources of society. The answer to that is that since the inception of the National Health Service the cost of medical services has declined in relation to national income and the cost of many other services.[1] On what ground, then, other than some nebulous neo-Rousseauism, could one argue that general interests have been prejudiced among the admittedly sectional interests at the Ministry?

To argue that the activities of the BMA and similar pressure groups prejudice democratic processes is to have a very innocent and academic notion of what democratic processes are all about. The relations between the Ministry and the BMA are a good example of both the limits and potentialities of such processes. Apathy (but apathy rooted in agreement) and technicality keep the bulk of their transactions on medical policy within the 'anonymous empire'; the power of the BMA as a 'veto group' undoubtedly gives it weight beyond its numbers, and perhaps also beyond its expertise. Yet there are important counterweights

[1] See Titmuss and Abel-Smith, *The Cost of the National Health Service*, 1956, *passim*.

against its power, most clearly of all when the Treasury intervenes; and, if we take the distribution of the national income as an index, these countervailing forces more than sufficiently do their job. Moreover, when a public interest may be said to exist concretely, not just abstractly, the normal machinery of responsible democratic government swings into action, exposing confidential transactions to publicity and tapping previously silent reservoirs of opinion. That, in any possible world, is all one can reasonably expect democratic machinery to do.

I rather think therefore, that political scientists who demand more light on pressure group activities demand it chiefly in their own interest as political scientists, and demand it not in any absolute sense but in a more easily accessible form. One can, to put the matter in a nutshell, get practically all the information one needs—to be an adequate citizen or an adequate political scientist—about medical politics in Britain, but not, as I know as well as anyone, without difficulty. The chief barrier, significantly, is not the conspiratorial silence of the pressure groups, but the institutionalized secretiveness of the administrative departments.

The Functions of Pressure Groups

In the language of contemporary 'functional' theory, pressure groups then are not manifestly dysfunctional in regard to democratic processes; they do not undermine them. They are in fact an inevitable term in the syndrome of an effective democratic system—alongside two-party systems and their functional equivalents, a wide range of fundamental political agreement itself, and a governmental machinery which can adjust rapidly to changing circumstances and act efficiently to realize shared social purposes. Indeed, it could be shown without great difficulty, if it were to the purpose here, that all these terms are related to one another as well as to the existence of effective democratic government. But do pressure groups really make any positive contributions to democratic government? Granted their inevitability, are they in any sense indispensable as well?

That pressure groups do useful work in the formulation and administration of specific policies like contemporary British medical policies is hardly open to question; I have tried to indicate these useful functions throughout the study. The BMA provides information to decision-makers, gives technical counsel, participates (however indirectly) in administration itself, helps to win and organize support, and acts as a communication channel for the grievances, large and small, which arise even in the best administered human enterprises. But groups like the BMA perform also functions of a more general character in democratic systems, functions not related to the contingent characteristics of any specific range of policy.

In the first place, pressure groups perform an important 'integrative' function in the political system. Any political system which values responsiveness to its members faces the problem of how to integrate the manifold goals of individuals (manifold even in the most consensual systems) into manageable ranges of alternatives for action. The widely varying perspectives and purposes of individuals must somehow be 'aggregated' if they are effectively to inform policy at all. We have always thought that this task of creating public opinions—integrated, supra-individual perspectives and goals—is primarily the function of political parties, and no doubt it is their pre-eminent function. But it is a function also of less fully politicized groups like the BMA. These groups aggregate specialized ranges of opinion on specialized subjects, and do so effectively in so far as their members identify themselves—their interests and goals—with those of the groups. Parties, in their very nature, tend to aggregate opinion on a very broad scale, rather infrequently, and for limited purposes, such as elections. This applies especially to parties like those in the Anglo-Saxon countries which must appeal to a very large electorate and are confronted less frequently with the need to define their position than parties in complex multi-party systems.[1] Pressure groups, on the other hand, constantly define opinion for government and do so on a level upon which parties only infrequently touch.

In certain political systems, therefore—especially two-party systems— pressure groups may be said to have still a second general function alongside their integrative function: a 'disjunctive' function. Two-party systems (perhaps any party system other than the most splintered of multi-party systems) tend perhaps to integrate political opinions all too well. In attempting to win mass support, necessarily from a large variety of groups, they do not so much 'aggregate' opinions (as Almond thinks[2]) as reduce them to their lowest and vaguest denominators, some-times distorting the perspectives and goals they seek to mobilize out of all recognition. One may doubt whether such systems could persist if groups did not have readily available outlets other than the parties through which to pursue their political goals.

The integrative function of parties in two-party systems is certainly important for the existence of stable governments and the simplification of issues at elections, so that easy choices may be made by the electors. The disjunctive function of pressure groups is equally important to prevent the alienation of groups from systems which persistently distort their goals; in that sense they are an indispensable element of stability

---

[1] I have in mind here the fact that parties in systems like the British tend to define their position chiefly in preparation for elections. Those in multi-party systems must also do so in the constantly repeated manoeuvring for coalitions.

[2] Almond, 'A Comparative Study of Interest Groups and the Political Process', *passim.*

in such systems.[1] Disjunction can, of course, go too far; but the crucial fact that pressure groups are mobilized to the greatest extent where political agreement has the greatest range, mitigates the potential divisiveness of pressure group politics.

In the light of this, the case for pressure groups in democratic systems is even stronger than I had previously made it. Democratic systems seem to work most effectively, from the standpoint of action, where parties work least effectively, from the standpoint of representation. For in democratic systems parties must perform simultaneously two functions which are, on the evidence, irreconcilable: to furnish efficient decision-makers and to represent accurately opinions. The best way to reconcile these functions in practice is to supplement the parties with an alternative set of representative organizations which can affect decisions without affecting the positions of the decision-makers. This is the pre-eminent function of pressure groups in effective democratic systems, as the competition for power is the pre-eminent function of the parties.

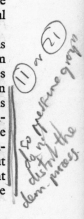

[1] In connection with this point, see the cogent remarks of R. T. McKenzie, *Political Quarterly*, Vol. 29, No. 1, p. 7 ff.

INDEX

Addison, Viscount, 104

Almond, Gabriel A., 162; report on interest groups and the political process, 8

American Bar Association, 21

American Farm Bureau Federation, 36

American Medical Association, 71, 92-3; compared with BMA, 51

Annual Conference of Representatives of Local Medical Committees, 59, 63

Annual Representative Meeting (BMA), 73; of 1948, 132; of 1951, 58-9. *See also* Representative Body

Anti-Saloon League, 9

Apothecaries Society, 51

Appointment Committees (NHS), 48

Association of Industrial Medical Officers, 51

Attitudes, towards BMA, 71-2; as determinants of pressure group politics, 16-17, 24, 27-9, 32-3; towards medical policy, 69-70; towards medical profession, 70; of medical profession towards trade union activities, 70, 107

Attitude groups, definition of, 9. *See also* Interest groups, Pressure groups

Attlee, Clement R. (Earl), 56

Barber-Surgeons Company, 50

Basic salaries, BMA opposition to, 131-2

Beer, Samuel H., 7, 10, 17, 28

Bentley, Arthur F., 22, 27, 152

Bevan, Aneurin, 55-7, 78-9, 80, 89, 90, 93, 98, 100, 103-4, 105, 107, 111, 118, 131, 138, 140

Beveridge Report, on Social and Allied Insurance, 74

Boards of Governors (NHS), 97

Brewers' Association, 27

British Medical Association, actuary of, 143; administrative expenses of, 45; Armed Forces Committee of, 84; Committee on Medical Legislation of, 41; Committees of, 45, 62-4; Compensation and Superannuation Committee of, 84; Conference of Honorary Secretaries of Divisions and Branches of, 59; early attitude towards politics of, 28, 40-4; failures in NHS negotiations of, 92-6; growth of political activities of, 41; and Home Office, 49; Hospital Junior Staffs Group of, 71; income of, 45; Medico-Political Committee of, 41; Medical Representation in Parliament Fund of, 76; Medical Reform Committee of, 41; membership of, 29, 44; and Ministry of Education, 49; and Ministry of Health, 48, 87-8; and Ministry of Labour, 49; and Ministry of Pensions and National Insurance, 49; and National Conference of Local Medical Committees, 47; National Health Service Defence Fund of, 107; and negotiations on NHS Act, 96-104; Occupational Health Committee of, 85; officials of, 45, 51, 61; organization of, 58-64; Parliamentary Agent of, 76; Private Practice Committee of, 84; public relations consultant of, 73, 76; Public Relations Department of, 71, 73; Registrars Group of, 117, 119, 120, 122; role of, in medical policy-making, 154-5; successes of, in negotiations, 96-112;

THE END